## About this book

This annual Prayer Handbook has become a vital par[t]
Methodist tradition. It draws together prayers from t
with those of contemporary writers; prayers for the lif
Church in Britain and Ireland with prayers from th
Church; prayers for individual use and prayers fo
worship. Thank you to all who have contributed to it,
especially to those of other Christian traditions whose
insights have enriched these pages.

## Methodist Year of Prayer

This Handbook and the Year of Prayer are a reminder that
God's mission to draw all people and all creation into the
community of the Kingdom must always be an integral part
of our life, prayer and worship. Spirituality and mission are
inseparable. In solidarity, we pray not only *for* but *with* those
who are mentioned, or who have written the prayers.
- Use your newspaper and include the day's news.
- Use the Lectionary readings on pages 74-79.

***Cover image***
© *LiquidLibrary*

## Pray without ceasing

Each time I have compiled and edited this handbook, and
when I write prayers, I am deeply conscious that Jesus said
we shall not be heard for our many words (Matthew 6.7-15).
The few words of prayer recorded as said by Jesus are
another indicator.

Prayer is to listen to God through our reading of the
Scriptures, reflecting upon what God's Word has to say to our
lives, our time and place; it is to hear God's voice in the daily
news, in the experiences and insights of people we meet
every day; it is to enjoy being with God in the silence. To 'pray
without ceasing' (1 Thessalonians 5.17) is more than words
and, as Charles Wesley reminds us (H&P 719 Part 2), it is to
'extend the arms' to include all people.

It is to walk so closely with God that God's loving presence,
God's anger at injustice and God's will for all people are like
the different movements of an orchestral symphony playing
deep within us and with which we interact. Our perceptions
keep changing, our vision grows, and we are renewed and
strengthened for the tasks we are called to do.

May we be confident that 'through our prayers and by our
lives' God's love flows out to heal and transform the
communities of the Church and of the world.

*Maureen Edwards*

***Prayer Handbook***
***Committee***
*Maureen Edwards*
*(Editor)*
*Susan Johnson*
*Michael King*
*Norman Wallwork*
*Sarah Middleton*
*Martin Stone*
*Michaela Youngson*

***Cover design***
***and layout***
*Lorna Lackenby*

# Pray without ceasing

## Pray without ceasing – helpful hints

The pace of life today is complex and time for prayer is limited. Yet it is possible to prepare short, easy to memorise prayer thoughts, for use anytime, anywhere:

- favourite texts from the Bible or lines of hymns ...
- words of praise, a thanksgiving, a complaint!
- Relevant, brief prayers, to meet tense situations in the family, workplace or between friends ...

> Lord, help me to control my temper in this situation ...
> Lord, help me to be understanding
>       when I meet Xy ... today.
> I must make important decisions that affect
>       other people: grant me wisdom and courage.
> Thank you, for my family ...
> Thank you, for my Church ...
> Thank you, for my friend Xy ...

Short, simple prayer thoughts as we move around the home, travel to work, wait for an interview, drink our coffee ...
And when, under stress, we cannot remember even the simple prayer we prepared, we cry out, 'Lord, I need your help.'

*Stanley Parsons, Supernumerary Minister, Dawlish*

When prayer is almost impossible
      short sentences
repeated over and over again can
      often be helpful.

Here I am, Lord. Here you are.
      That is enough.
Keep a tight hold on me, Lord.
      I am weak and afraid of falling.
Hold me in the centre of your love –
      Lord Jesus.
Give me strength for today
      and hope for tomorrow.

*From* Food for Thought *by Gill Girt, who suffers from Myalgic Encephalopathy (Chronic Fatigue Syndrome)*

Lord, we say too much.
Help us to pray without words.
May the pictures in our minds,
      conjured up by the words on
            these pages,
be coloured by the brush strokes of your
unceasing love. Amen

*David Halstead, Sheffield District Chair*

## Call to worship

Pray without ceasing.
Rejoice in the presence of God.
Draw on God's strength;
    God's gracious love in Christ,
    enfolding peace,
    forgiveness for our sins.

Pray without ceasing.
Bring our hopes and dreams,
    joy and laughter,
    sorrows and tears,
    regrets;
a kaleidescope of words,
    ever changing – reshaping
    and reflecting our needs.
Lay them before
    an unchanging God.

Pray without ceasing
to God who is more willing
    to listen
than we are to pray.
Come in awe and wonder,
    in deep humility,
    with reverence.
No words can capture
    the mystery and majesty
    of God who created us.
In stillness and silence, pray;
for silence too is prayer.

*Jan Grimwood,*
*Local Preacher, Oxford Circuit*

## Adoration

Loving God, you draw light out of
darkness and coax beauty from chaos.
*(silence)*
You spread rainbow promise across time
and space. **Amen**

You make music and song in the sounds
of creation.
*(silence)*
You paint pictures of glory in the stars
and the clouds. **Amen**

You scatter the sparks of creative
initiative.
*(silence)*
You penetrate madness with wisdom
and truth. **Amen**

You weave patterns of hope in the
traumas of history.
*(silence)*
You lavish your love-gifts in boundless
excess. **Amen**

You grace us with peace and with warm
hospitality.
*(silence)*
You welcome each person regardless of
race. **Amen**

You invite us to dine at the table of plenty.
*(silence)*
You fill us with faith, with hope and with
joy. **Amen**

You come to us, believe in us, embrace
us, and stay with us,
**for you are our God,**
**our redeemer and friend.**

*Tom Stuckey,*
*President of the Methodist*
*Conference, 2005/6*

## Confession

Lord of all life,
we use thousands of words each day
yet so few of them are about you.
**Forgive us.**

We see and meet many people
but forget that in them we could be
    meeting you.
We busy ourselves in so much
    rushed activity
that we blank out the silence within.
**Forgive us.**

Help us to retune our lives
to the silent music of your beckoning
presence. Amen

*Tom Stuckey*

Lord God,
you are the centre of our lives.
You never leave us.
You are our constant companion,
wherever we are
and whatever we are doing.
So often we forget this
and try to live without you.
Forgive us.
Enter our hearts and minds now,
    and be our focus today
and everyday.
Help us to live prayerfully, praising you
and serving you in everything.
In Christ's name we pray. Amen

*Elaine Turner, President of the Women's
Network of the Methodist Church, 2004/5*

## Intercession

God of all lands,
we pray for places in the news…
places of disaster,
devastation and death…
and for places forgotten.

God of all peoples,
we pray for people in the news…
people whose lives have been disrupted,
people in doubt and despair,
people who feel forgotten.

Reconciling God,
we pray for all who feel guilt
at the hurt they have caused to others,
or because of the way they have
mismanaged the lives and
    trust of others.

Forgiving God,
we pray for all who have feared or
    neglected to challenge
    corruption and evil;
and for ourselves, as we have
    compromised the values of
    your Kingdom.
Give to all your people integrity,
    healing and hope
and enable us to share these gifts with
your damaged world.
In Christ's name. Amen

*Audrey Stanley, Local Preacher,
Christchurch and Lymington Circuit*

Creator God,
who turns darkness into light,
    and sorrow into joy,
take our ignorance and teach us
    your way,
our weakness and give us
    your strength,
our prejudice and show us
    your truth,

so that we may be at one
    with your will
and our lives be refashioned
into something beautiful for you.

Lord Jesus Christ,
who transforms the lives of those
    who trust in you,
we pray with all who suffer
because of the greed or wickedness
    of others.
Show us how we can be as Christ
    to them,
challenging injustice,
and offering hope where there is
    despair.

Holy Spirit of God,
who inspires and energises
    your people,
enable, encourage and equip us
to serve one another
so that together
we can make a difference in your world.
Amen

*Alison Judd, President of the Women's*
*Network of the Methodist Church, 2005/6*

## The voice of prayer

In the wonders of creation
as in the beauty of the sunrise,
**the voice of prayer is never silent.**

In the noise and laughter of family life
as in the solitude and loneliness we know,
**the voice of prayer is never silent.**

In the tedium of our daily work
as in the joyous discoveries of each day,
**the voice of prayer is never silent.**

In the sorrow and suffering of this world
as in the signs of love and compassion,
**the voice of prayer is never silent.**

In all the world, in each continent

and island
as in this place and at this moment,
**the voice of prayer is never silent.**

We offer our voices
and our silence,
    our love and our lives,
    to you in ceaseless prayer.

*Stephen Poxon, Chair of the North*
*Lancashire District*

## Closing prayers

Holy Spirit,
Spirit of the Living God,
you breathe in us,
on all that is inadequate
and fragile.

You make living water spring even from
our hurts themselves,
and through you, the valley of fears
becomes a place of wellsprings.

So, in an inner life
with neither beginning nor end,
your continual presence makes new
freshness break through. Amen

*Sri Lanka, World Council of Churches*
*Worship Book 1998*

God our Father,
send the gift of the Holy Spirit
    upon your Church
that its unceasing prayer on earth
    may be united
with the intercession of Christ
    in heaven:
may your people daily
    increase in their devotion to you
    and in love for their neighbours;
through Christ our Lord. Amen

*Norman Wallwork, Superintendent Minister,*
*Weston-Super-Mare*

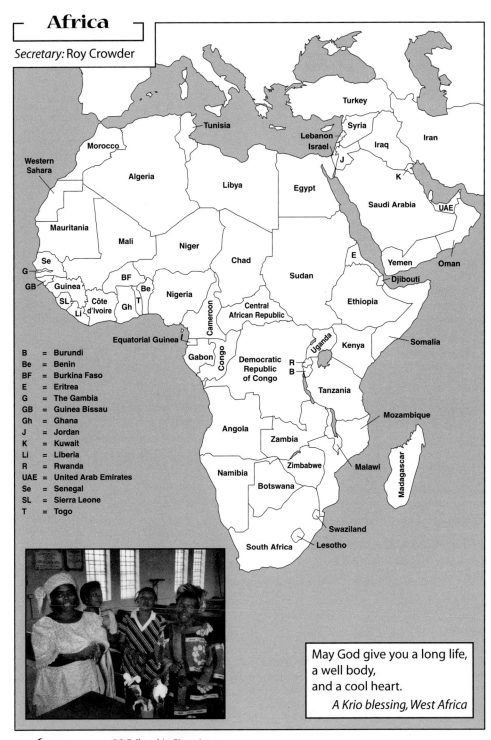

# Africa

Secretary: Roy Crowder

Turkey

Tunisia

Morocco · Syria

Lebanon
Israel · Iraq · Iran

Western
Sahara

Algeria · Libya · Egypt

Saudi Arabia · J · K · UAE

Mauritania

Mali

Niger · Chad · E

Se · Sudan · Yemen · Oman

G

GB · BF · Be · Djibouti

Guinea · Gh · Nigeria · Ethiopia

SL · Côte
d'Ivoire

Li · T

Cameroon

Central
African Republic · Somalia

Equatorial Guinea

Gabon

Congo

Uganda · Kenya

Democratic
Republic
of Congo · R · B

Tanzania

Angola · Zambia · Mozambique

Namibia · Zimbabwe · Malawi · Madagascar

Botswana

Swaziland

South Africa · Lesotho

B = Burundi
Be = Benin
BF = Burkina Faso
E = Eritrea
G = The Gambia
GB = Guinea Bissau
Gh = Ghana
J = Jordan
K = Kuwait
Li = Liberia
R = Rwanda
UAE = United Arab Emirates
Se = Senegal
SL = Sierra Leone
T = Togo

May God give you a long life,
a well body,
and a cool heart.

*A Krio blessing, West Africa*

*BO Fellowship, Sierra Leone*

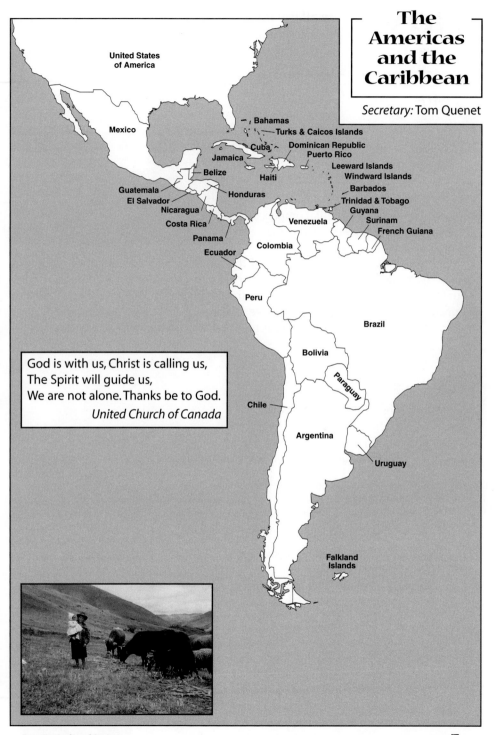

# The Americas and the Caribbean

*Secretary:* Tom Quenet

United States of America

Mexico

Bahamas

Turks & Caicos Islands

Cuba

Jamaica

Belize

Haiti

Dominican Republic
Puerto Rico

Leeward Islands
Windward Islands

Barbados

Guatemala
El Salvador
Nicaragua

Honduras

Trinidad & Tobago
Guyana
Surinam
French Guiana

Costa Rica

Venezuela

Panama

Ecuador

Colombia

Peru

Brazil

Bolivia

Paraguay

Chile

Argentina

Uruguay

Falkland Islands

God is with us, Christ is calling us,
The Spirit will guide us,
We are not alone. Thanks be to God.
*United Church of Canada*

*Peru Agricultural Project*

# day 1

**Be all my love, O God**, all my hope and all my striving; let my thoughts and words flow from you; may my daily life be in you, and every breath I take be for you; for Jesus Christ's sake. Amen

*John Cassain, c.360-435*

*Praying with all creation*

O Lord our God,
you have created a beautiful, complex and diverse world to provide a stage that enriches the drama of everyday events. We thank you for the myriad elements of the natural world that together produce a sense of place and local distinctiveness. They are markers in the history and geography of our lives. We give thanks for the rare and the commonplace, the treasured scene and the great wonders of the world. Preserve in us a sense of awe and respect for our surroundings, and a desire to live unselfishly in balance with nature.

*Rodney Shaw, Principal Conservation Officer,*
*Mole Valley District Council, Surrey*

Christ with outstretched arms,
we remember you,
lest we fold our arms in an attitude of defeat or indifference,
saying to ourselves, 'It is not our problem.'

Christ with hands pierced by nails,
we remember you,
lest we use our hands to grasp and to hoard,
saying to ourselves, 'It is not our problem.'

Christ with tired and dusty feet,
we remember you,
lest we choose the easy path,
saying to ourselves, 'There is no other way.'

Jesus Christ, whose words and works were one,
grant that our lips and our lives may agree.
In your name, by the power of the Spirit,
and for the glory of God,
send us out to bring the Kingdom in. Amen

*Caroline Ainger, Methodist Relief and Development Fund*

**Give thanks** for the emerging vision of a reshaped District that will be able to respond more effectively to opportunities for ministry and mission in the diverse areas being served.

**Please pray** for the District Strategy Group as it looks at ways in which the Church engages with the economic and social development (including proposals for a major increase in housing provision) in the Thames Gateway and in the London-Stansted-Cambridge 'corridor'.

**Lord, teach us to pray:**
 when there is much to do
 and when we need just to be;
 when we are full of hope
 and when we despair;
 when we can see clearly where you are leading
 and when we struggle to discern the way;
 at all times
 and in all our circumstances,
Lord, teach us to pray.

*Ermal Kirby*

**We pray** for those who have left the church
that they may not lose their awareness
of God's loving presence…
for all who search for meaning…

## UNCEASING PRAYER

 As light and darkness caress the face of the earth,
so your life-giving Spirit, O God,
touches the hearts, minds and lips
of your people
evoking prayer, praise and petition.
May my prayer
be added
to the universal chorus of concern and celebration,
which hallows your name,
and anticipates the coming
of your Kingdom. Amen

*Tom Stuckey, President of the Methodist Conference*

## London North East District

*Chair:*
Ermal Kirby

*Secretary:*
Kathleen Burrell

*President of British Methodist Conference:*
Tom Stuckey

*Vice-President:*
John Bell

*Youth President:*
Kevin Jones

*Women's Network President:*
Alison Judd

*General Secretary:*
David Deeks

*Assistant Secretary:*
Ken Howcroft

*Co-ordinating Secretaries:*
Ruby Beech
Anthea Cox
David Gamble
Jonathan Kerry
Peter Sulston

*Diaconal Order Warden:*
Susan Jackson

*Give thanks for the order and beauty of created things*

# day 2

**Steer my ship, good Lord**, to your quiet harbour. There may I be safe from the storms of sin and conflict. Direct my course and shelter me when the waves are high. Guard me when the sea is rough, and in every danger grant me your comfort and peace; through Christ our Lord. Amen

*Basil the Great, 330-379*

## Praying with Christians in West Africa (1)

---

### The Gambia District

*Chairman:*
p Norman Grigg°

*Mission Partners:*
p   Elaine Woolley°
ad   John Woolley

*Experience Exchange:*
Douglas and Christine Baker

*Scholarship Student:*
Sally Forster (in Britain)

### Sierra Leone

*Methodist President:*
Francis Nabieu

**Give thanks** for the remarkable faith of African peoples.
**Pray** for growing congregations and ecumenical co-operation in **The Gambia**;
for the continuing work of well-established mission projects in agriculture, education and medical work;
for the leaders of the Church as it gradually moves towards autonomy.
**Pray** for all in **Sierra Leone** who are seeking to bring healing and reconciliation after so many years of conflict and suffering;
for health workers trying to maintain basic health care and for people struggling to rebuild churches, schools, homes and places of work;
for the staff of the Nixon Memorial Hospital at Segbwema, establishing and developing work again;
for plans to extend mission activity into neighbouring Guinea.

**Lord, I long for your people in Africa –**
for the day when children can to go to school and university without struggling and worrying about every term's fees;
when parents will live long enough to see their children grow up and find jobs as they do in Britain and Ireland;
when parents will be able to support their families without the worry of how to provide for the next meal.
I long for the day when Africa will be free
from war, AIDS, poverty and malaria.
Lord, I long for your people in Africa.

*David and Rhoda Nixon, Mission Partners, Zambia*

As we remember those who have few possessions
but who are rich in faith,
may we learn the secret of Christ's way:
that it is in losing ourselves that we find life.

**We give thanks** for new insights and enthusiasm for the gospel brought to us by the many overseas visitors who throng our churches, and for renewal through Alpha Courses and the introduction of the 'Walk to Emmaus' programme.

**We pray** for the new West Dublin Circuit set up in response to the huge new housing developments;

for the courage to continue to break new ground as we respond to the need in the hearts of all people, both old and young;

for those who champion the rights of people from other lands.

**Dublin District**

*Superintendent:*
Ken Wilson

*Secretary:*
Donaldson Rodgers

---

**Give thanks** for the Avenue – a newly renovated church on the Castlefield estate in High Wycombe and for the Deacon coming to serve the community.

**Pray** for the staff and students of Christ the Sower – a new ecumenical school in Milton Keynes;

for the children and residents of Sneha Home in Bangalore supported by Haddenham Church.

**London North West District**

*Chair:*
Anne Brown

*Secretary:*
Andrew Hollins

*Mission Partners:*
Bernardino° and Elizabeth Mandlate (Mozambique)

*At SNEHA Home, Bangalore
Sneha – the Tamil word for 'friend'.*

## Coming and going

Dear Lord, our life is a constant
 coming and going.
Day by day we come and go; come and go...
We come to you for forgiveness and grace;
and we go out to a hurting world with this message of love.
Forgive us when we come and, because of selfishness or fear,
we forget to go out.
Forgive us when we go out without first coming to you. Amen

*Ken Wilson*

*President of the Methodist Church in Ireland:*
Brian Fletcher

*Secretary of the Irish Conference:*
Winston Graham

*Secretary of MMS (Ireland):*
Robert Russell

*President of Methodist Women in Ireland:*
Phyllis Watters

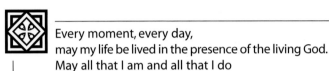

Every moment, every day,
 may my life be lived in the presence of the living God.
  May all that I am and all that I do
 be an offering of prayer and praise.
May I see the world more clearly
 and learn to love more dearly
through the prayers I offer to the living God.

*Anne Brown*

*Give thanks for the resources of the earth*

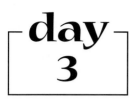

# day 3

**Come, source of eternal Light**. Come, giver of eternal Life. Fill our hearts with your love, fill our mouths with your praise and fill our lives with your presence; now and for ever. Amen

*Symeon the New Theologian, 949-1022*

Praying with Christians in West Africa (2)

## Bénin

*Methodist President:*
Simon Dossou

*Mission Partner:*
Sp  Liz Rose

## Côte d'Ivoire

*Methodist President:*
Benjamin Boni

*Scholarship Students:*
Esmel Amari°
   (in Cameroon)
Jean-Marc Athangba°
   (in Morocco)

## Togo

*Methodist President:*
Felix Adouayom

*Scholarship Students:*
Gerard Atohoun
   (in Senegal)
Benjamin Gaba°
   (in Edinburgh)
Pascal Loko (in Britain)

**Give thanks** for faithfulness in the midst of difficulties.
**Pray** for peace and stability in each of these countries;
for courage and wisdom for all who lead the Churches;
for the continuing recovery of the Methodist Church **Benin** after a period of internal dispute;
for the work of theological institutions in **Côte d'Ivoire**, including the Faculté de Yaounde, and for young ministers beginning their ministry in complex and challenging situations;
for Assoupoe Delphine Akolly (NMA) in **Togo**, who is responsible for projects offering medical care and support for people living with HIV/AIDS and raising awareness of this issue in the community;
for the prophetic ministry of the Churches in Togo where oppression and exploitation continue.

## Make poverty history

Loving God,
we pray with the peoples of Africa,
who cry out for fairer Trade Laws,
for a more just distribution of the earth's resources:
that governments may choose the best solutions
to end poverty
and protect the environment;
for new laws to stop larger businesses making profits
at the expense of the world's poor;
that the richer nations and banks
will continue to cancel debt and increase aid;
and that we ourselves
may be willing to pay more for our food
so that our brothers and sisters in other parts of the world
may receive a fair price for their labour.
**Lord, you made us one family: show us how to care.**

**Give thanks** for the gifts of older people throughout the District and their commitment to mission and service.
**Pray** for the ministry to the newly elected Parliament; for the Church's concern for the welfare of homeless people.

## Life-threatening illness

*How does one pray for those who are ill? Acceptance of the condition can become a gateway to receiving help and prayer. Often this takes time, effort and determination not to lose hope.*
Lord Jesus, this condition comes like an ill wind, and I fear where it will end. Draw close to me those whose skill and faith can help. Then in the power of your resurrection, may love cast out fear, light shine in the darkness and the days of peace begin. Amen

*Malcolm Knowles, a deacon in the Aldershot, Farnborough and Camberley Circuit*

## Depression

**We pray** for people suffering deep depression:
for psychiatrists and counsellors,
community psychiatric nurses and social workers,
for 'care in the community',
that we too may offer friendship and support.
**Lord, you made us one family: show us how to care.**

## Bereavement

When words stick in the throat and tears blind us,
then, Lord, send your Strengthener to help us rise again,
remembering the Nazarene
    who knew loneliness and suffering
and yet always advanced your Kingdom.
Equipped afresh may we continue
    to further the realm of right relationships. Amen

*Bernard Dowding, a bereaved Supernumerary, Dorchester*

**London South West District**

*Chair:*
John Swarbrick

*Secretary:*
David Chapman

*Mission Partners:*
John° and Faith° Nyota, Cherie and Kim (Kenya)

Praised be the Holy Spirit,
    who is present
in the depths of our being
    and burns away
the sufferings of our life
    in the fire of his presence.
*Brother Roger of Taizé*

*Give thanks for the gift of human life*

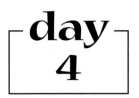

# day 4

**Grant to me, O Lord**, a gentle spirit open to you; a generous mind open to all others and a loving heart worthy of being your dwelling place; through Christ our Lord. Amen

*John of Kronstadt, 1829-1908*

Praying with Christians in West Africa (3)

---

**Equatorial Guinea**

*Methodist President:*
Manuel Sañabá Silochi

**Ghana**

*Methodist Presiding Bishop:*
Robert Aboagye-Mensah

*Mission Partners:*
ad/ed Ian and Diana Bosman

**Let us thank God** for the testimony of more than 150 years of Methodism in **Equatorial Guinea**, for peace and for the discovery and extraction of oil in our country.
**Let us pray** that this will benefit all the population;
for a spiritual revival in our Church, the reconciliation of people with each other and a commitment to work together;
that ordained pastors may be able to respond to the spiritual needs of believers.

*Prospero David Sharpe, a Methodist minister in Equatorial Guinea*

**We thank God** for peaceful elections in **Ghana** in December 2004 and for small groups praying as they queued to vote.
**We pray** for President John Kufor, that a corrupt-free and just society may emerge;
for children for whom there are no school places or money to pay the fees;
for the sick who suffer at home while hospitals have empty beds;
for rain so that the 2004 water shortages will not be repeated;
for peace in the Francophone countries on our borders.

Pray for Ransford Sowah and Peter Salia (NMAs) in Wa, using Bible study to encourage new development projects;
for the Revd Dr Symonds Botchey (NMA), combining evangelism with free medical treatment;
for Charlotte Baah (NMA), providing training for unskilled girls and young mothers;
for Dr Archer Turpin (NMA), working at Lake Bosontwe to improve health and safety awareness in this remote area.

**Akwaaba! Welcome!** – is heard everywhere in Ghana. Here people matter most and always have time to share.
Lord, may we be as welcoming in Britain.
Forgive us when we exclude people and may those of us who are busy set aside time for others.

*Diana Bosman, Mission Partner, Ghana*

## Midlands and Southern District (Ireland)

**Give thanks** for the consistent and faithful witness of the Church as it seeks to minister and seize opportunities in ever changing circumstances;

for marginal numerical growth for the third year in succession.

**Pray** for new residents, that they may find a warm welcome and have opportunity to play a full part in the life of the Church;

for those who are concerned about their future and fear deportation;

for areas where there is large-scale housing development and movement of population that the Church may have the vision and resources to respond to the challenge.

*Superintendent:*
Paul Kingston

*Secretary:*
Noel Fallows

## London South East District

**We thank God** for commitment to the gospel across our wide and varied region;

for signs of new life and hope in unexpected places.

**We ask God** for wisdom, understanding, patience and guidance in the implementation of the new London Regional District;

for strength to sustain our vision of the Kingdom in situations with serious demands on resources, financial and pastoral;

for courage to do new things for God;

for grace and blessing on Roger Cresswell, the new District Chair.

*Chair:*
Roger Cresswell

*Secretary:*
Russell Bates

God our Redeemer,
who called your Church to witness
that you were in Christ
reconciling the world to yourself,
help us so to proclaim the good news of your love
that all who hear it may be reconciled to you;
through Jesus Christ our Lord. Amen

*From the Methodist Worship Book*

Loving God, in our commitment to building communities of justice and peace, help us to remember the hospitality of your grace. In our discerning of your will for us, help us to discover your presence in unexpected places. In our daily duty and discipleship, help us to be joyful. In all things, may we reflect in some small way the glory of your presence and purpose.

*Keith Davies, Chair of Manchester and Stockport District*

*Give thanks for creative vision and inventive skill*

# day 5

**Be with us, Lord**, to defend us; within us to refresh us; around us to protect us; before us to guide us; behind us to encourage us and above us to bless us; for your own name's sake. Amen

*Celtic, 10th century*

Praying with Christians in West Africa (4)

## Cameroon

*Moderator of the Presbyterian Church:*
Nyansako-ni-Nku

*Scholarship Student:*
Divine Ekoko° (in South Africa)

## Nigeria

*Methodist Prelate:*
Sunday Mbang

*Mission Partners:*
p/ad   Diane Blair
d      Hans and Mary Van den Corput, Marcel and Maurice
d/m    Julian and Polly Eaton (+CA)
p/ad   David Keenan (+CA)

*Scholarship Students:*
Aderonke Adesola (in Britain)
Innocent Ekeke° (in Britain)

**Give thanks** for unity and peace in **Cameroon** since Independence and for the growth and vitality of the churches. **Pray** for the Church, giving thanks for those within it who are helping to make it an instrument of social protest and reform; for Hans Ekema Njoh and James Ako-Egbe (NMAs), working to improve the financial basis of the Church;
for the unemployed that they may find opportunities to earn a living in all honesty;
that the Government may be able to drive away corruption and selfishness and work for the benefit of all.

*Edward Sakwe WCBP Cameroon/Leicester*

**Pray** for **Nigerians** coping with few resources, high costs and political unrest, and that the values of past traditions may not be lost in the process of development and change;
for the Revd JU Ogi (NMA), manager of Bethesda Hospital which provides health care in a scattered rural area;
for Deaconness Ronke Oworu (NMA), Women's Work Programme Officer, and Mrs Morin Bamgbose (NMA), ensuring the smooth running of the Prelate's Office.

Gracious God, we thank you for another year in which to journey with you. We acknowledge your love for our country, and that in spite of all the difficulties we are still together in unity.
We pray for the National Political Reform Conference, which we hope will address the issues that divide us. Keep us in peace, strengthen our faith and unite us in love; in Jesus' name. Amen

*Bishop M K Stephen, Secretary of the Nigerian Conference*

O almighty God, we humbly ask you
to make us like trees planted by the riverside,
that we may bear fruits of good living in due season…
for Christ's sake. Amen

*from a Nigerian prayer: Morning Noon and Night (CMS)*

**We give thanks** for the rich diversity of people and places that are encompassed in the 22 circuits of the District.

**We pray** for people who work in the name of the Church, lay and ordained, across the District;

we remember particular situations where resources are scarce while needs are great.

We pray for those who dare to be 'new church' in new situations.

### Birmingham District

*Chair:*
Bill Anderson

*Secretary:*
John Nodding

*Mission Partners:*
Florence Deenadalayan° (CSI) Stephen° and Angela Mullings, Stephanie, Angelique and Georgianne (MCCA) th Israel° and Leelal Selvanayagam, Arul, Ani and Sunil (CSI)

*Inner city Birmingham*

## For understanding between faiths

Creator God,
parent of all diversity,
help us to delight in the perceptions of your nature
   as they shift and change
and save us from the violence of warring creeds.
May we learn by the encounter with the mystery of your being
to put off the grave clothes of certainty
and Strip the Willow of discovery.
May we recognise our partners in the dance
as skilful seekers, equal artists,
not rival advocates of competing schools.
Because there is no victory to win
may we draw from the wells of mutual wisdom,
share the songs of salvation we have learned
within our individual families
and make a harmony of praise
to celebrate one God in Unity.

*Bishop Michael Hare Duke, Perth*

## On learning to contemplate

Lord, there are many layers to our prayers. Often we are distracted by our well thought words. Help us to learn to dwell with you in our thinking. Help us to set ourselves aside. Help us to see the world through your eyes – to move towards experiencing your mind. So may our response be harmonised by your love which makes all things new. Amen

*Peter Fox, retired GP and Local Preacher, Tavistock*

*Give thanks for God's care for people*

17

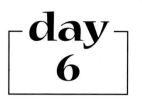

# day 6

**Grant to us, O Lord**, to pass this day in gladness and peace, without stumbling and without stain, that reaching the eventide victorious over all temptation, we may again praise you, the eternal God, blessed over all things now and for ever. Amen

*Mozarabic Sacramentary, 10th century*

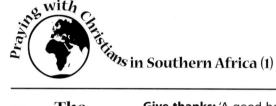 in Southern Africa (1)

---

## The Methodist Church in Southern Africa

*Methodist Presiding Bishop:*
Ivan Abrahams

**South Africa**
*Mission Partner:*
sd Eileen McDonald

*Experience Exchange*
Roy Escott

**Botswana**

**Lesotho**

**Mozambique**

*Scholarship Students:*
Mozambique Group Training (in Mozambique and South Africa)

**Namibia**

**Swaziland**

**Give thanks:** 'A good heart is also a good way of celebrating your victory. I celebrate it when I see people I fought with and the people who tortured me working together.'

*Mkhuseli Jack, who was detained and tortured under Apartheid*

**Pray** with the MCSA as it seeks to build meaningful relationships that transcend racism and all forms of discrimination, to make a vigorous response to the HIV/AIDS crisis and to become a Church which acts in solidarity with the poor;
for Joseph Wentzel and Morgan Raboshaga (NMAs) who are working in the Mission Unit to develop a clear understanding of the progress and needs of mission projects;
for Thuthu Diamini (NMA), working with children in an area where HIV/AIDS and child-headed households are prevalent;
for NCH Action for Children projects, especially in the Richards Bay area of KwaZulu Natal and in Eastern Cape, near Umtata, where there are many child-headed families.

Let us renew our personal commitment to Jesus Christ and seek to grow in grace and in love for God, one another and the world.
Let us participate in God's mission... in partnership with the wider Church and community.
Let us celebrate our diversity and the gifts God has given to each of us; let us support each other, challenge each other and pray for each other.
God bless this Africa which is our home.
Give us grace to follow Jesus the healer,
Jesus the peacemaker,
Jesus the Saviour of the world,
Jesus the Lord of all life.
Restore us and make your face shine on us
that we may be saved.

*From the Charter of the Mission Congress, November 2004*

**Bolton and Rochdale District**

*Chair:*
David King

*Lay Secretary:*
Val Pownall

**Give thanks** for a sense of working together across the District and with numerous partnerships to enable the mission of Christ to be shared by more and more people.

**Pray** for our developing links with South Africa;
for closer co-operation in mission and ministry between the Littleborough and Rochdale Circuits and between the Prestwich and Whitefield and Radcliffe Circuits;
that all circuits continue to take up the opportunities of Local Strategic Partnerships in their boroughs;
for the new Chair and Secretary of this District.

Gracious and loving God, who calls us to global mission,
pour out your Spirit upon us that we may
 faithfully hold before you the needs of the world.
Help us to share our resources,
 to learn from each other
 and to capture a vision of all your creation as one.

*Keith Garner*

### Space for hearing
Gracious God,
through prophets, preachers and people of faith,
 your message of love has been told.
Your word has dwelt among us
 but often we have failed to hear or understand it.
Help us to create space in our prayers
 to hear your voice
Help us to pause in our activity
 to see glimpses of your love at work in the world.
In Jesus' name. Amen

*Michaela Youngson,*
*Secretary for Pastoral Care and Spirituality*

Creator God, fill me with your creative, loving Spirit.
Help me to take that love to all I meet today.

Lord Jesus Christ, fill me with your healing and forgiveness.
Help me to take that healing and forgiveness to all I meet today.

Holy Spirit, fill me with your power.
May that power be with me everywhere I go today.

*Josette Crane, Local Preacher, Bristol*

*Give thanks for God revealed in the prophets and the Scriptures*

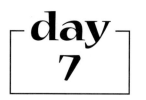

# day 7

**Let me desire you, O Lord**, with my whole heart. Thus desiring you, may I seek you; seeking you, may I find you; finding you, may I love you; loving you, may I be parted from those sins which separate me from you; and this I beg for Jesu's sake. Amen

*St Anselm, c.1033-1109*

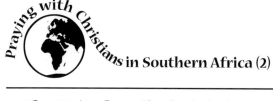 in Southern Africa (2)

---

## The United Church of Zambia

*Synod Bishop:*
Mutale Mulumbwa

*Mission Partners:*
p   David° and Rhoda Nixon, Samuel and Christopher
ad/ad  Brian and Georgina Payne (+C of S)
sp   Wendy and Michael Curtis

## Zimbabwe

*Acting Methodist Presiding Bishop:*
Margaret James

*Mission Partners:*
ed   Jonathan and Isobel Hill, Stephen and Susanna
rt   Pat Ibbotson

*Scholarship Students:*
Walter Magagula (in Britain)
Solomon Zwana° (in Britain)

**Give thanks** for the work of mission schools and hospitals and for all who are involved in the struggle against poverty and HIV/AIDS. **Pray** with all who long for rain, for strength and wisdom as Church and other organisations co-ordinate relief work in **Zambia** (80% live in absolute poverty and many are refugees from Angola and the Congo);
for the Government struggling with scarce financial resources;
for all who suffer HIV/AIDS (one-in-four of the population);
for all who minister in this context and for circuits struggling with a shortage of ministers. In rural areas one minister may have 60 or more churches and no transport. In urban areas one minister may have to care for 3-4000 members.

**Pray** with the peoples of **Zimbabwe**, with all who long for change and those campaigning on their behalf, for a willingness of those in power to listen to the voice of the people;
for a resolution of the land issue and for the restoration of human dignity;
for all whose homes have been demolished by the security forces and for Churches and other agencies who are caring for them;
for those forced to become refugees, now living far from their families and homeland;
for Zimbabweans who have come to live in Britain...
Pray that the Church, by preaching and example, may be a force for reconciliation and peace.

### An African Prayer

O Father God,
I cannot fight this darkness by beating it with my hands.
Help me to take the light of Christ right into it.

*Light of the World Prayer Book (Church Mission Society)*

**Give thanks** for vision and active outreach.

**Pray** for the circuits as they plan for the future and get used to having fewer ministers;

for young people growing up in a rural situation with limited employment opportunities in agriculture.

**Enniskillen and Sligo District**

*Superintendent:*
Eric Duncan
*Secretary:*
Philip Agnew

---

**Give thanks** for District study and training opportunities at Wesley College, including our developing Resource Centre;

for the work of our Training and Development Officer, Susan Graham, and the Training Team she co-ordinates.

**Pray** for ministry among the homeless, especially our Midland Road Centre in Bristol and Barry Penn its chaplain;

for ministry in local prisons and our prison chaplains – Dilwyn Edwards (Horfield), Donald Blackmore (Eastwood Park), Dinah Whittall (Erlestoke), Vernon Godden (Gloucester), Roger Bayliss (Leyhill), Chris Day (Shepton Mallett), Richard Jones (Ashfield).

**Bristol District**

*Chair:*
Ward Jones

*Secretary:*
Carrie Seaton

*Mission Partners:*
Ajay° and Latika Singh, Shekinah and Sharon (CNI)

## Times of crisis

Loving God,
when we see disasters, may your presence help us,
for without it we will reach breaking point.
We search for you, for your mercy, when we are weak
    and unable to face the challenges of the world.
We pray with the poor and those who suffer,
for those whose faith grows in times of crisis,
for they know that you are with them in their need.
Give us your vision so that we remain in Christ and he in us,
and may we serve you for ever. Amen

*Ajay and Latika Singh, Shekinah and Sharon, WCBP/Swindon*

A new day, a new start, new possibilities...
Lord, help me to be still in body, mind and spirit,
to create a space where I can encounter you;
where together we can explore questions you may have for me;
where you can help me prepare for the people I will meet
and the places to which I will go;
where you can give me joy to rejoice,
strength to cope and compassion to encourage ...
As I go, may I know your presence within and around me. Amen

*Ward Jones*

*Give thanks for God's supreme revelation in Christ*

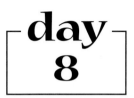

# day 8

**Behold and acknowledge in me**, O Good Shepherd, a lamb of your own flock, a sheep of your own fold, a sinner of your own redeeming and an inheritor of your heavenly kingdom; and this for your own name's sake. Amen

*Aelred of Rievaulx, 1109-67*

 in East Africa

---

## Kenya

### (Tanzania and Uganda)

*Methodist Presiding Bishop:*
Stephen Kanyaru M'Impwii

*Mission Partners:*
n  Barbara Dickinson
p  Andrew° and Sheila Moffoot, Timothy, Samuel and Joseph
d  Connie Pullan (+CA)
d  Claire Smithson
sd  Jeana Scofield

*Experience Exchange:*
Siobhan Scully

*Scholarship Students:*
John Ataya° (in Britain)
Susan Kimathi (in South Africa)
Mwenda Mburugu° (in Britain)
Alice Mwila (in Britain)
Geoffrey Lugwire (in Britain, from Uganda)

**Give thanks** for work begun by the Government to create a more just society.

**Pray** for ministers and leaders throughout **Kenya**, facing new challenges in a time of great change;

for the Meru North Disability Community Centre and its work with children over a wide area (part of a wider initiative to raise awareness of disability issues and provide help for individuals);

for the HIV/AIDS Palliative Care Programme at Maua Hospital (two-thirds of the patients are women). Pray that people may gain confidence to admit openly that they are infected and benefit from treatment, and so encourage others to seek help;

for the AIDS Ministry course at St Paul's United Theological College where students are trained to develop resources to fight the disease and reduce its impact, and to reflect on the theological challenge: where is God in all this?

for the new MA Course in Islam to equip ministers to enter into dialogue with their Muslim partners.

Pray for churches in **Tanzania** as they seek to move towards becoming more self-reliant;

for Mrs Esther Betongyeza (NMA), Coordinating Women's and Youth Work in the **Uganda** Mission, establishing church programmes and small income generating projects.

## World Church in Britain Partnership

We pray for the families
who leave their home and culture to serve in Britain,
often shocked by our indifference to prayer,
our neglect of the Bible and our loss of traditional values...
We pray that as we listen to each other
we will hear your voice, O God of all peoples,
speaking to us in new ways, calling us to repentance,
broadening our horizons and enriching our lives.

**Give thanks** for the mission partnership link between the North and East District of the Sri Lankan Methodist Church and the South Wales District;

for the ministry of the Wales Training and Development Officers: Luke Curran, Gwenllian Roberts Knighton and Michael Wilson and for students undertaking Foundation Training;

for the many young people here who are committed to Christ.

**Pray** for the Valley Circuits in South Wales as they adjust to changing circumstances;

for the development of co-operation between English and Welsh medium work and for the appointment of an Evangelism Enabler for Cymru and North Wales Districts;

for ministry in the holiday town of Llandudno, the town centre of Wrexham, the university city of Bangor and the industrial chaplaincy at Airbus UK.

As we celebrate the centenary of Revival in Wales (1904-5), we remember that it began through the prayers of young men and women. Their prayers were answered, lives were transformed and so we pray that we may repent and turn to the Lord again. Through our prayers, Lord, help us to understand your will for us as Christians here in Wales.

*Patrick Slattery*

For the beauty of the sunrise over the hills,
for the changing patterns of the sky,
for the constant movement of the sea,
for the grandeur of snow-capped mountains,
**we praise you, O God.**

For the diversity of humankind in all its strength and weakness,
for the richness of culture and context,
for the challenge of living in changing times
and the opportunities to serve in our time,
**we praise you, O God.**

For the sense of your abiding presence,
for the power of prayer to encourage and enable,
for the ability to dream dreams and bring them to reality,
for the privilege of being co-workers with you
    in building your Kingdom,
for glimpses of heaven on earth,
**we praise you, O God.**

*Barbara Bircumshaw*

### South Wales
*Chair:*
William Morrey

*Secretary:*
Graham Illingworth

### Cymru
*Chair:*
Patrick Slattery

*Secretary:*
Dennis Griffiths

### North Wales
*Chair:*
Barbara Bircumshaw

*Secretary:*
Trevor Pratt

*Mission Partners:*
Edson° and Sammie Dube, Nomthandazo and Nozipho (Zimbabwe)

### Y Cyngor ('The Council')

*Y Llywydd ('The President'):*
Philip Barnett

*Executive Officer:*
Chris Mainwaring

*Treasurer:*
Anthony Gregory

*Give thanks for the obedience of Christ to the Father's will*

# day 9

**O good Jesus, radiant in your glory** and tender in your compassion, cherish me, I pray, as one of your family; embrace me as your lover; rule me as your subject and welcome me as your friend, now and for ever. Amen

*Hildegard of Bingen, 1098-1179*

 **Praying with Christians in South America (1)**

---

## Brazil

*Methodist Bishop:*
João Alves de Oliveira Filho

## Uruguay

*Methodist President:*
Oscar Bolioli

## Argentina

*Methodist Bishop:*
Nelly Ritchie

*Mission Partner:*
p      Sue Jansen°

## Colombia

*Methodist President:*
Juan Cardona

*Scholarship Student:*
Juan Guerrero°
(in Puerto Rico)

**Give thanks** for people sustained in the struggle.

**Pray** for all who seek to live the gospel among homeless families and street children in each of these countries; for a co-operative (supported by Network) in **Brazil**, training women in dressmaking and other skills to raise their income; for Cleonice de Queiroz Nery and José Carlos do Prado Ramos (NMAs), working with street people and for Maria Moreira Lima (NMA), accessing the rights of young people in Brazil.

**Pray** for the development of ministry and leadership in **Uruguay** as many of the most able move to the USA to find employment; for a project (supported by Network) to train women to lead workshops and help other women in crisis situations; for Anibal Siccardi, Heber Cardosa and Marcos Rocchieti (NMAs).

Pray for the people of **Argentina** and the Churches there, very slowly recovering from the economic crisis of 2001; for the training of lay leaders and presbyters; for Gabriela Amaya (NMA), providing new educational and devotional resources for the Church and Jorge Ostapzuck and Patricia Fernandez (NMAs), evangelists in remote areas;

for evangelistic and social outreach in **Colombia**; for churches used as feeding centres for children; for William and Rocío Llanos (NMAs), developing new work in the city of Medellin.

Let us rely on the presence of the Spirit
    who will teach us what to say.
Let us be neither fearful nor anxious;
    his grace will provide for each day.

*Santiago Stevenson (USPG Encounter Feb/May 2005)*

**Give thanks** for 'Sustainable Communities', a partnership between the churches and secular agencies promoting environmental awareness and local action;
for 'Called to Serve' a new course enabling people to develop their discipleship in the church and in the world.
**Pray** for small congregations finding a new understanding of what it means to be the church;
for presbyters and deacons exploring new patterns of ministry;
for new possibilities where all seems lost!

### Cumbria District

*Chair:*
David Emison

*Secretary:*
Keith Burrow

## Prayer for peace

Lord, I want to give you thanks for all that I have.
I ask you to satisfy people's hunger and enlighten every family.
God, I want you to bring peace to all the world!
Loving God, many thanks for the life that you give us,
for games, school, nature, animals and health...
I would like every boy and girl to know and love you.
God, thank you for being real.
*Dios, gracias por EXISTIR... Amen*

*Veronica Lago Bottezini, a 10 year old girl, Brazil*

**We pray for families facing difficulties:**
trying to cope with children's demands on a low income;
families where a parent or child is disabled;
mothers facing an unplanned pregnancy,
making difficult choices, sometimes alone,
for lone parents (one in five of all families)...
**Lord, you made us one family: show us how to care.**

Faithful God,
when all is not well
and when, in our searching, we find too easy answers,
then help us to trust:
in your justice and truth,
    your mercy and forgiveness
    and your steadfast loving-kindness.
We ask it in the name of the crucified and risen Christ.
Amen

*David Emison*

*Give thanks for the value Christ gave to human labour*

# day 10

**O consuming fire, O Spirit of love**, O Word incarnate burn in my heart, purge my soul and dwell within me, now and for ever. Amen

*Elizabeth of Schonau, d.1184*

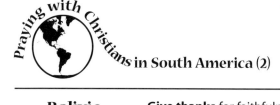 **Praying with Christians in South America (2)**

---

## Bolivia

*Methodist Bishop:*
Carlos Poma

## Chile

*Methodist Bishop:*
Pedro Grandon

*Mission Partner:*
p Thomasina Elers
p/sd  Alison Facey°,
   Chris Esdaile
   and Luke

*Experience Exchange:*
Helen Read

## Peru

*Methodist Bishop:*
Marco Ochoa

rt  Margaret° and
   Aldo Valle

## Ecuador

*Methodist Bishop:*
Salomón Cabezas

**Give thanks** for faithfulness and courage when life is hard.
**Pray** for the Methodist Church struggling, in these countries, with issues of management and limited resources;
for work with indigenous peoples in remote areas;
for Marina Tenorio Siles (NMA) in **Bolivia**, working with CLEM to provide Primary Health Care;
for Benjamin Avendano (NMA), co-ordinating the Church's projects and finances in **Chile**;
for a programme (supported by Network) in **Peru**, to combat discrimination against women and girls who have moved to the cities as domestic workers;
for the ministry in **Ecuador** of small health care and community development projects in a poor area of Latacunga;
for the church in Pacto, ministering to remote, scattered communities and helping people to develop computer skills;
for Eduardo Vega, David Murgueytio and Rodolfo Lemos (NMAs), developing outreach in the community.

**We pray for Mission Partners**
who have left home for the sake of the gospel
to live in new places,
sometimes remote and hard,
entering a different culture,
learning to speak another language,
feeling alone and vulnerable
in volatile political situations,
in the midst of suffering and conflict,
identifying with poverty,
getting used to a limited supply of water
but knowing God has called them there
and God is with them.

**North West District (Ireland)**

*Superintendent:*
Harold Agnew

*Secretary:*
Alan Macaulay

**Give thanks** for the new life and fresh vision of a small rural church at Cavandoragh, Co. Tyrone.
**Pray** that more may hear the call both to local preaching and the ordained ministry;
for fresh vision to move from maintenance to mission ministry.

**Channel Islands District**

*Chair:*
David Coote

*Secretary:*
Stephen Robinson

**Give thanks** for the new and ambitious NCH Youth Project in Guernsey, providing facilities for young people needing accommodation and a safe place;
for the deepening and growing awareness of God following the Jersey 24/7 week of prayer.
**Pray** for Methodist Homes on Jersey and Guernsey as they expand their work into new areas of care;
for the ongoing life of the Church as it responds to the challenge to reshape itself for mission and for the chapels on Alderney and Sark in their important ministry to visitors and local people;
for those across the islands who seek to stand side by side with those in need and to 'make poverty history'.

Lord, we stand side by side with all who travel, for we are a pilgrim people. We rejoice that you are the way of love and the way to life. Whatever the journey, we walk in your company. Show us your way, so that through us and beyond us all places may reflect more truly your love for all. We pray in confidence: 'may your Kingdom come on earth as it is in heaven'. Amen
*Caroline Homan, Channel Islands*

*5000 people gather on the beach in Jersey in solidarity with Tsunami victims*

## The voice of God
In stories of Jesus; in stories of the apostles; in stories of the saints; in stories of my friends; in stories of the poor; in the stories of those who work for peace and justice... I hear the echo of God's voice. And sometimes when I listen hard I hear that echo in my own story. It rebounds, reverberates, mixes and meshes with all those other stories, and in its midst I hear a voice that calls me on to live a faithful life.
So we pray in the midst of life:
Speaking God,
may we hear your voice echoing in our lives.
Grant us ears that hear,
that we may know your way and our path. Amen
*Andy Lyons, student at Queen's College, Birmingham*

*Give thanks for the strength Christ gives to his disciples*

27

# day 11

**Look upon your servant, O Lord**, weak in faith and asking for your strength; cold in heart, but seeking the warmth of your love; assailed by doubt but longing to trust you; abounding in sin, yet begging to be filled with your righteousness; now and for ever. Amen

*Martin Luther, 1483-1546*

*Praying with Christians* in Central America

---

## Belize and Honduras District
of the MCCA

*District President:*
David Goff

*Mission Partner:*
p Janet Corlett°

## Panama and Costa Rica District
of the MCCA

*District President:*
Mario Nicolas

## Guyana District
of the MCCA

*District President:*
Barrington Litchmore

## Guatemala

*Methodist President:*
Tomás Riquiac Ixtán

## Mexico

*Methodist Bishop:*
Raul Rosas González

**Give thanks** for communities of hope, evangelical fervour and strong faith.

**Pray** for the Churches facing difficult questions and ministering to families who struggle to survive;

for work with children living on the streets;

that traditional values may not be lost in the pursuit of development;

for ministry to the growing number of people with HIV/AIDS, especially in **Belize** which has the highest number infected in Central America;

for Pedro Valdez (NMA) in **Panama**, involving young people, making new members and holding workshops on intra-family violence, and for Margaret Johnson (NMA) who, through education, ministry and chaplaincy work is strengthening the Church's witness in the community;

for Andella Shannon Moore (NMA) working with young people in Guyana;

for the people of **Guyana** whose sugar estates are threatened with closure because they do not yield big profit. This would change the whole social life of the people and lead to untold hardship for thousands of employees;

for Edith Molina Valerio (NMA), who is National President for Christian Development in **Mexico**.

Lord,
if this day you have to correct us
put us right not out of anger
but with a mother and father's love.
So may we your children
be kept free of falseness and foolishness.

*Prayer from Mexico (source unknown)*

**We give thanks** for two different experiments in café-style church at Chester and Kidsgrove – appealing to those looking for fresh ways of being church.

**We pray** for the International Prayer Conference, Methodists in Renewal, planned for Stoke-on-Trent in the summer of 2006; for the developing 'Bridge Centre' (Burslem Mission Circuit) adapting a school to serve as a worship centre and 40 studios for young, design-led start-up businesses and a community focal point for service providers.

### Chester and Stoke-on-Trent District

*Chair:*
John Walker

*Secretary:*
David Scott

*Mission Partners:*
Jimione° and Miriama Kaci, and Salanieta (Fiji)

### Lord, we turn to YOU

snatching a moment to dream at the bus stop
saving the time from frustration and waste,
spending a second to stay with each letter
sending our thoughts without more thoughtless haste,
seeing the snowdrop and viewing hope through it,
sharing such insight communion we taste.
So we pause often for peace and for Presence.
May we relax in your love through such prayer.

*John Walker*

### Creator God,

in the intricate traceries of a single snowflake
    we recognise the genius at the heart of creation.
In the relentless force of a biting blizzard
    we wrestle with the awesome power of creation.
The welcome rays of spring sunlight bless our upturned faces,
    yet burning heat causes famine's cruel blight.
We struggle again to make sense of your plan
    for our complex world.
Grant us the wisdom to accept
    that we will not be given answers to all our questions.
Give us confidence to know that to challenge the way things are
    is part of our call to discipleship;
and help us to maintain a sense of awe
    in the face of everyday miracles. Amen

*Michaela Youngson, Secretary for Pastoral Care and Spirituality*

God does not give an answer to all our questions
but in Jesus, God enters into the heart of the questions.

*Leonardo Boff, Latin American theologian*

*Give thanks for the call to follow Christ*

29

# day 12

**Rule over me this day, O Lord**, and lead me in the way of righteousness. Put your word into my mouth and your truth into my heart. Let me think only what is good and honest and help me to discern your will in what I do. May I be alive at all times to the promptings of your Holy Spirit; through Christ our Lord. Amen

*Jacob Boehme, 1575-1624*

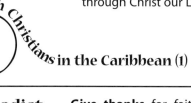

*Praying with Christians* in the Caribbean (1)

---

## Methodist Church in the Caribbean and the Americas (MCCA)

*Connexional President:*
George Mulrain

*Scholarship Student:*
Oral Thomas° (MCCA)

## Leeward Islands District
of the MCCA

*District President:*
Selwyn Vanterpool

## South Caribbean District
of the MCCA

*District President:*
Victor Job

*Mission Partners:*
p    Elaine° and Ewart Joseph

**Give thanks** for faith in the midst of crisis and faithful discipleship in a changing society.

**Pray** for churches in these Districts responding to the changing patterns of family life, domestic violence and HIV/AIDS;

for people still rebuilding their livelihood, homes and churches after Hurricane Ivan swept through the region in 2004;

for those caught up in a culture of drugs and crime;

for the District Resource Centre in the **Leewards Islands**, providing lay training, financing consultancy and media services, and counselling;

for Stephane Brooks (NMA), providing pastoral leadership for the Guadeloupe/Martinique Mission;

for Marlene Britton-Walfall (NMA) in the **South Caribbean**, as she co-ordinates the Church's new school curriculum material and Tanya Conliffe (NMA) co-ordinating a Church Renewal Programme in Barbados;

for Karen Ambo-Christian (NMA), working with the **Caribbean Conference of Churches** to raise awareness and support families coping with HIV/AIDS.

Loving God,
    deepen within us a spirituality of hope:
        that we may hold on to all that affirms life,
and develop a stronger sense of community,
a spirit of solidarity:
we are our sister's and our brother's 'keeper'.
So may we learn to combat violence and injustice,
to protect the weak and vulnerable among us,
and to hear your voice speaking to us through them.

**Cornwall District**

*Chair:* Christopher Blake

*Secretary:* Celia Phillips

**Give thanks** for the energy, enthusiasm and vision seen at our recently inaugurated District Youth Synod and for the work of our District Youth Enabler;

for the excitement and commitment of all who attend our annual residential training event for those who work with children.

**Pray** for the development of an ecumenical youth congregation in Perranporth and that the MAYC 6T national celebration (to be held in Cornwall in September 2005), may lead to further growth in our ministry with young people;

for the work of our recently appointed Evangelism Enabler and the District Evangelism Team.

## Following Christ

Our Father, as we are encouraged to pray continually, fill us with your Holy Spirit, because we long to communicate our deep love for you, and to discuss our concerns.

Through the Spirit, remind us that you designed us and gave us the desire to serve and follow you at all times and in all places. Help us in the way we treat others to make our lives a continual prayer to you. As Jesus showed us your love for everyone, however bad, so may our lives reflect that love.

Go on loving us, Lord God, and accept our love, as you did yesterday, and will do today and tomorrow. Amen

*Chantelle Wiseman (15 years old),*
*Cornwall District Youth Synod Representative*

*Prayer wall at Methodist Youth Conference 2004*

Dear God,
thank you that we can meet together with other young people;
that we can help to change the world through our debates;
for the volunteers who helped to make the Conference
    run so smoothly;
thank you for inspiring us to do your work.

Help us to continue on our journey thinking about the future;
help us to guide others as you have guided us;
help us in our daily lives to worship;
help us as we continue to meet at weekends
    to build and strengthen our faith. Amen

*Emma Parker, Rebecca Pitt and Joseph Walker,*
*members of the planning team, and delegates to*
*the Methodist Youth Conference 2004, Basingstoke*

*Give thanks for opportunities of work and leisure*

# day 13

**Defend us, O Lord**, with your heavenly grace, that we may continue yours for ever and daily increase in your Holy Spirit more and more, until we come to your everlasting Kingdom; through Jesus Christ our Lord. Amen

*Book of Common Prayer, 1552*

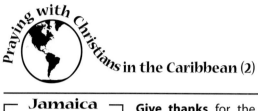 Praying with Christians in the Caribbean (2)

## Jamaica District
of the MCCA

*District President:*
Byron Chambers

## Bahamas and Turks and Caicos Islands District
of the MCCA

*District President:*
Raymond Neilly

*Mission Partners:*
p Eddie° and Susan Sykes, Jonathan and Thomas

*Experience Exchange:*
Elizabeth Leicester

## Haiti District
of the MCCA

*District President:*
Raphael Dessieu

## Cuba

*Methodist Bishop:*
Ricardo Pereira Díaz

*Scholarship Students:*
Cuba Group Training (in Cuba)

**Give thanks** for the significant contribution of Methodist schools in this region, in spite of few resources;
that the largest number of candidates for ministry come from Haiti whose poverty is 'a challenge to the whole of humanity';
that men and women with HIV/AIDS hear the gospel and come to faith in a society which often rejects them.

**Pray** for families recovering from last year's hurricane (over 1700 people died in Haiti and many lost crops and possessions);
for justice and peace in the divided country of **Jamaica**;
for the many people in **Haiti** who have a growing sense of helplessness and who long for peace and democracy;
for the future of the 105 Methodist schools which are among the best in the country;
for Jean Seguere (NMA), an auditor who is working to improve the accountability and management of resources and for Donnette Parris-Lataillade (NMA), Administrative Assistant to the District President;
for Cesar Blanc Castellanos (NMA) in **Cuba**, providing training in local lay leadership and for Humberto Fuento Sánchez (NMA) who is working on a new worship book for the Methodist Church in Cuba.

 Dear God, you are not just a name featuring on currency notes, or a being invoked at State functions. You are alive in nature: in whistling birds, waves breaking onto our beaches, towering mountains, scenic valleys... We encounter you in Christ and in the exciting cultures of our region. May nothing – sickness, death, natural disaster, or any other adverse situation – ever prevent us from acknowledging your continual presence, through your Son, our Saviour and Friend, Jesus Christ. Amen

*George Mulrain*

**North East District (Ireland)**

*Superintendent:*
Aian Ferguson

*Secretary:*
Trevor Jamieson

**Give thanks** for this area of outstanding natural beauty with its hills, glens, meadows and coastline. God alone is Lord, who gives life to everything and whose mercy and grace are seen in Jesus Christ.

**Pray** for the District as it ministers in a changing time; for churches as they ascertain afresh their purpose and mission; that our worship, witness and work will be wholehearted, all to the glory of God and for the good of people.

**Darlington District**

*Chair:*
Graham Carter

*Secretary:*
Paul Wood

**Give thanks** for the new Linthorpe Road Centre in Middlesbrough, maintaining worship and developing service to the community and for the new church at Normanby, providing a fresh source of inspiration for the neighbourhood congregation.

**Pray** for the new Cleveland and Danby Circuit serving urban and rural communities over a wide area and the 'Helping Hands' scheme in Redcar enabling elderly people to live at home; for the Eastbourne project in Darlington, where the circuit has taken over the running of the local church to develop links with a more deprived community in the town; for the newly appointed District Mission Enabler supporting and encouraging the circuits in a wide range of mission activity.

**We pray for the homeless,**
for those who beg on our streets:
for discernment and compassion in responding to their need;
for centres and projects offering shelter.
Remind us, loving God, that you speak to us
    through the poorest and most vulnerable…
**Lord, you made us one family: show us how to care.**

Lord, when I am busy, remind me that all life can be a prayer, but save me from the excuse that I don't need space and quiet to remember you;
when I have time and space, remind me that you are in the silence, but save me from restricting you to special times and places;
when pain confuses me and I cannot find you in busyness or in quiet, remind me that you are with me in my confusion and pain;
for the sake of the One who worked with his hands, sought peace away from the crowds and died in pain and loneliness, even Christ our Saviour. Amen

*Graham Carter*

*Give thanks for the truths God has enabled humanity to discover*

33

# day 14

**Give us grace, O Lord**, to be not only hearers of the word, but doers also; to be not only lovers of your gospel, but those whose lives are transformed by it; to be not only those who profess our faith, but also those whose lives proclaim it, day by day; through Christ our Lord. Amen

*Thomas Brecon, 1513-1567*

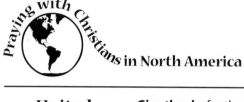

## Praying with Christians in North America

---

### United Methodist Church (USA)

*Ecumenical Officer to the Council of Bishops:*
William Oden

### The United Church of Canada

*General Secretary:*
Jim Sinclair

**Give thanks** for those who challenge injustice and exploitation.
**Pray** for churches coping with reduced membership;
for sensitive debate where there are major disagreements within the Church on social issues;
for the Council of 130 Bishops who pledged themselves 'to build bridges of understanding ... to overcome the gulf that divides the nation and the world'. Although the Church's social principles are in direct contrast with the President's stated beliefs, the UMC believes that this is an opportune time to be in dialogue with him about the nation and the world.
Pray for the Interfaith Neighbours' Programme in Portland, Oregon:
* accompanying Muslim men and women who feel threatened when they go out alone,
* rabbis and pastors hosting get-to-know-you dinners for Muslim leaders
* and Jewish lawyers working with Muslims.

Dear God,
open our hearts
so that we may feel the pain of those who are victims
    of senseless acts of violence.
Unclench our hands
so that we may reach out to one another.
Open our lips
that we may speak for justice, wholeness, health and safety
    for all people.
Unclog our ears
to hear your agony in our inhumanity.
Open our eyes
to see you in the midst of the horror that touches our world.
Be with us we pray. Amen

*United Church of Canada*

**We give thanks** for the ways in which our District is being challenged to meet the needs of people today.

**We pray** for the exciting developments at Glemsford and other villages where people are responding to God's call;
for courage to take up the opportunities that are being created for new work with children and young people.

## Relationships

Loving God,
thank you that you did not make us to be alone,
but gave us other people to share our lives:
parents, children, partners, families, friends, colleagues;
those with whom we share our days, our hopes, our fears;
people for whom we care and those who care for us.

We remember those for whom today will be difficult
because someone they love is absent, ill, or dying,
or because their lives or relationships are in a mess.

We think of those whose closest relationships have been
    abusive,
those who feel betrayed, ignored, unloved...
and those for whom love has died and who are drifting apart.

Help us to respect each other, especially when we disagree,
to be honest and acknowledge when we get things wrong,
to meet each other more than halfway,
and teach us how to forgive and how to accept forgiveness.

*David Gamble, Co-ordinating Secretary*
*for Legal and Constitutional Practice*

### East Anglia District

*Chair:*
Graham Thompson

*Secretary:*
Grahame Lindsay

*Mission Partners:*
Frank° and Gabi
Aichele (Germany)

Lord, you invite us to be a people of prayer.
May we be among those who speak to you,
    listen to you
    and respond to you.
Help us to act upon all that you share with us
so that we may become more like Jesus, day by day.
Amen

*Graham Thompson*

*Give thanks for the intercession of Christ in heaven*

# Asia

*Secretary for Asia and
the Pacific:*
Christine Elliott

*Slum Children in the Philippines*

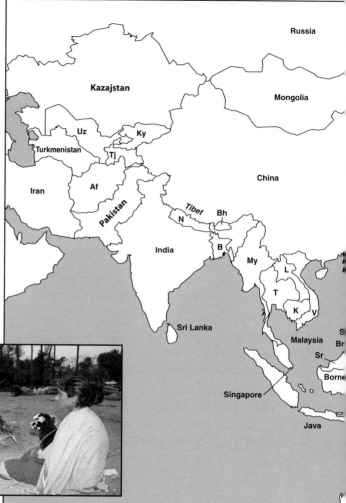

*Post-Tsunami*

Iraq is steeped in history. It is the site of the Garden of Eden, of the Great Flood and the birthplace of Abraham. Tread lightly there.

*Lieutenant Colonel Tim Collins to his troops*

We can do no great things,
Only small things with great love.

*Mother Teresa of Calcutta*

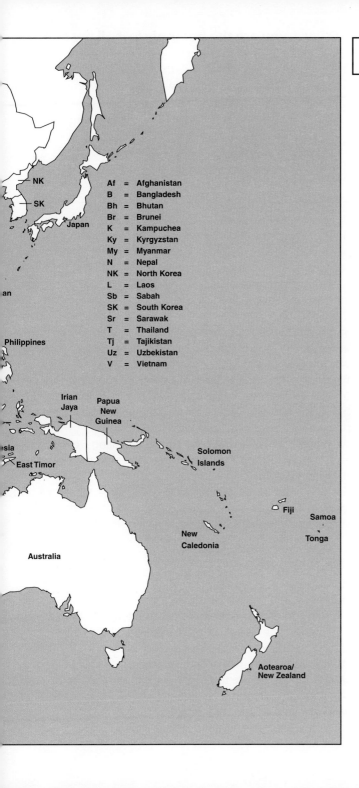

NK

SK

Japan

an

Philippines

| | | |
|---|---|---|
| Af | = | Afghanistan |
| B | = | Bangladesh |
| Bh | = | Bhutan |
| Br | = | Brunei |
| K | = | Kampuchea |
| Ky | = | Kyrgyzstan |
| My | = | Myanmar |
| N | = | Nepal |
| NK | = | North Korea |
| L | = | Laos |
| Sb | = | Sabah |
| SK | = | South Korea |
| Sr | = | Sarawak |
| T | = | Thailand |
| Tj | = | Tajikistan |
| Uz | = | Uzbekistan |
| V | = | Vietnam |

Irian Jaya

Papua New Guinea

sia

East Timor

Solomon Islands

Fiji

Samoa

New Caledonia

Tonga

Australia

Aotearoa/ New Zealand

# day 15

**O Lord, you are the beginning of all my good**, the wellspring of all my love and the source of all my freedom. Let your grace work on in me, that your will may be done through me, and that I may always rejoice in your presence; now and for ever. Amen

*Mary Ward, 1585-1645*

 Praying with Christians in the Middle East

---

## Israel/ Palestine

*Ecumenical Accompaniment Programme in Palestine and Israel (EAPPI):*
*September Departure:*
Gerald Conyngham
Jan Sutch Pickard

*December Departure:*
Marissa Johnson
Mary O'Regan

## Jordan

## Lebanon

**We pray** with Christians – now only 1.5% of the population of the Holy Land (in 1948 they were 18%) – for freedom for their people who are being forced into ever-shrinking pieces of land.
**We pray** with Sabeel, an ecumenical grassroots movement seeking to promote unity and reconciliation and to promote international awareness of the issues that divide this now unholy land...
and with the Churches we pray for an end to the culture of violence, suicide bombings, overwhelming military force and wanton destruction.
We pray with all whose land was confiscated and whose olive trees were destroyed to build the wall of separation which now blocks the access of Palestinians to their olive groves, markets, pasture, water, schools, hospitals...
We pray with all who made their living by selling woodcarvings and pottery to tourists and whose shops are now closed and their streets empty...
We pray with all who long for peace – Jews, Christians and Muslims, Palestinians and Israelis – and with other communities in conflict throughout the world:

---

### For world peace
Loving God,
forever yearning that your people may turn to you
so that you may lead them like a shepherd,
we pray for the healing of all scars of war and conflict,
for the settlement of disputes and reconciliation,
that rough places may become plains.
May your people live to enjoy the fruits and the shade
of trees they planted in their youth
and to celebrate the coming of your Kingdom
of justice and peace in all the earth. Amen

**Give thanks** for the significant rise in the Government's Overseas Aid Budget and its partnership with Christian Aid and CAFOD projects.

**Please pray** for a closer working together of the three Island Circuits and for continuing opportunities for ministers to be involved in the Island's schools.

**Isle of Man District**

**Rheynn Ellan Vannin Yn Agglish Haasilagh**

*Chair:*
Stephen Caddy

*Secretary:*
Malcolm Peacock

## Walking prayer

First there was a call
to us, in the midst of daily life,
to set out on a journey – not escaping –
challenged to live otherwise in the world: *'Follow me.'*

At the roadside,
in the market place, on doorsteps,
in the gutter – encounters
which changed us for ever: *'Do you want to be healed?'*

Along the way,
conversations which were not easy –
questioning our assumptions,
threatening our status:
*'The first will be last, and the last first.'*

Resting on hillsides and in homes,
sharing food for the journey,
friendship, stories, laughter –
being known in the breaking of bread:
*'This is my body ... you are my body.'*

Weeping for the city,
whose stones cry out against injustice,
walking its streets, carrying a cross
to the place of execution: *'You must take up your cross.'*

Running from the tomb,
scarcely believing our eyes –
full of the good news,
challenged to travel on:
*'Go and tell my brothers ... Go into all the world.'*

**God, who walks with us –**
**give us imagination, courage, grace**
**to be companions of the Way.**

*Jan Sutch Pickard,*
*former Warden of the Abbey in Iona and EAPPI (page 38)*

*Give thanks for the joy of human love and friendship*

# day 16

**Teach us, O Lord**, to love your house the best of all dwellings; to love your scriptures, the best of all books; to love your sacraments, the best of all gifts; to love your saints, the best of all company and in so loving to come to know you more and more, both in this life and in the world to come. Amen

*John Donne, 1571-1631*

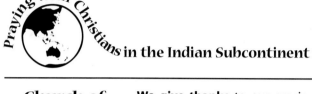

**Praying with Christians in the Indian Subcontinent**

## Church of Bangladesh

*Moderator:*
Michael Baroi

*Mission Partners:*
t/ed   David and
    Sarah Hall and
    Rebecca
sd James Pender
r   Gillian Rose
n   Shani Sedgwick
(all joint appointments with CofS, CMS, USPG)

*Rosemary Symonds with Bangladeshi women*

## Church of Pakistan

*Moderator:*
Alexander Malik

**We give thanks** to our gracious and loving God for all the support we received from around the world when the flood caused so much suffering to the people of **Bangladesh**;

for the work which is developing among very poor, disadvantaged people in the Dhaka slums (many are being helped and empowered);

for Dr and Mrs Sarkar (NMAs), working at Bollobhpur Hospital in a very remote rural area of great need.

We pray for our country. There is so much political turmoil and violence that we fear for the future. As a Church in this globalised world, may we grow and develop to meet the needs of our people, especially the young.

*Michael Baroi, Bangladesh*

**Pray** for Alice Malik (NMA), Co-ordinator of the Women's Development and Service Programme in Pakistan, addressing the very real needs of women caught up in the sex trade.

Heavenly Father, Creator of heaven and earth,
bless your churches in **Pakistan**
who spread your name among those who do not believe in you.
Give them the 'helmet of salvation'
and the 'sword of the Spirit', which is your word,
so that they may fight against all that is 'wicked'.
Give them the power that you gave to Paul
when you turned him into a new person so that
he devoted his whole life to the ministry of the gospel.
May Christians in Pakistan never give in to despair.
Give them your righteousness and truth.
Grace be with all of them who love our Lord Jesus Christ. Amen

*Jennifer Haroon Dass, Pakistan/Redhill*

**Give thanks** for the dedication of the new Jennymount Church after the fire.
**Pray** for the expected developments at Belfast South and the East Belfast Mission.

### Belfast District

*Superintendent:*
Kenneth Best

*Secretary:*
Donald Ker

---

**Give thanks** for a substantial legacy which has enabled the funding of a District Evangelism Enabler post for five years.
**Pray** for the Revd Beverly Hollings as she becomes District Evangelism Enabler and for the new Learning and Development Group as it seeks to co-ordinate and enhance learning opportunities across the District.

### Leeds District

*Chair:*
Michael Townsend

*Secretary:*
Richard Oldroyd

## Emmanuel

Listen to me, O God: I am in a whirlwind,
a seeker after truth in a hostile world.
Calm me, restore my faith in humankind.
Be a still point, piercing the cloud.
I respond to the evils of the day as I see them,
and hope that my response will influence others for good.

Vulnerable God,
you have created a world of rich variety,
and mysteriously made yourself known to us
through peoples of many cultures.
You are with me in my weakness and isolation.
Increase my love for you,
and renew my passion and faith.
You have always been there for me.
Your love is constant. Emmanuel!

*Based on Psalm 86 – by a group at the Methodists
for World Mission (MWM) Conference 2004*

God our Saviour,
your care for us has neither measure nor end.
Help us to respond to your love in our daily living;
    to pray more fervently,
    to share our faith more openly
    and to seek first your Kingdom and its righteousness;
through Jesus Christ our Lord. Amen

*Michael Townsend*

*Give thanks for our families and friends*

# day 17

**Be a light, O Lord, to my eyes**, music to my ears and contentment to my heart. Be sunlight in my day, food at my table and rest to me in the night. Take into your hands my body and my soul, my freedom and my life. Let me rejoice to be about your business and let me live to your praise and glory, now and for ever. Amen

*John Cosin, 1594-1672*

Praying with Christians in India

## Church of North India (CNI)

*Moderator:*
James Terom

*Scholarship students:*
Amiya Das° (in Britain)
John Thamvakumar°
(in Britain)

## Church of South India (CSI)

*Moderator:*
Peter Sugander

*Experience Exchange:*
Mary Eden

*Scholarship student:*
Barnabas Absalom°
(in Singapore)

**Give thanks** for ministry among dalit communities (800 million people), that those who are marginalised, isolated and trapped by poverty find refuge and welcome in the church.
**Pray** for the freedom of all to religious and social rights;
for the rebuilding of communities along the east coast devastated by the Tsunami;
and for continued peace between India and Pakistan.

**Pray** with the **CNI** in its concern with the issue of child labour and for women's rights;
for the AIDS Teen Peer Educator Programme set up in schools to encourage awareness and prevention;
for Vivek Samuel Massih (NMA), working in the Delhi Diocese to motivate and support young people and families in slum areas.

**Pray** for Charlet Rajan (NMA), Director of the Arulagam Hospice of the **CSI** which provides residential care for terminally ill and destitute HIV/AIDS patients and their children;
for the Women Workers' Training Centre, training women in leadership, new skills, family welfare and Christian living.

Where the mind is renewed by the Spirit;
where people are united to God's call and not fragmented
　　by the narrow walls of regionalism and denominationalism;
where lifestyle does not allow contradiction
　　and tireless involvement leads to transformation;
where engagement in God's mission is supported
　　by personal involvement and the mind is open
　　to ever widening thought and action –
let the Churches of India AWAKE.

*From a prayer by Enos Das Pradhan, General Secretary (CNI)*

**Give thanks** for the Mission-Shaped Leadership Course, an ecumenical initiative, training leaders and emerging leaders for mission and offering fresh expressions of church.

**Pray** for 'Integration Lincolnshire', a new initiative in Boston which offers support and guidance to the thousands of economic migrants who live and work in the area, for the ministry of Helen Freeston and Alan Robson, and for the outreach and hospitality of our rural chapels to guest workers; for all who are taking forward the Anglican-Methodist Covenant and are exploring with our ecumenical partners what it means to be an effective Christian presence;

for the Revd John Tomlinson, Ecumenical Co-ordinator for Mission for Churches Together in All Lincolnshire.

**Lincoln and Grimsby District**

*Chair:*
David Perry

*Secretary:*
Mark Childs

## Imaginative dialogue

Holy God,
in this moment,
I offer to your creative and redeeming hands
all the textures and colours
of my living and imagining.
Held in your wisdom and compassion
may they find their place
in the ever-changing collage of your grace,
a reminder in every moment
of your abiding love.

*Liz Smith, Lincoln and Grimsby District*

As a painter sees deeply and responds creatively, so may my seeing be an imaginative dialogue with you, O God whose gaze is loving and whose artistry is eternally hopeful.

*Words and image © David W Perry*

Lord,
I live two lives.
One is dedicated to you – the other to me!
I try to balance them but know this is grounded in folly.
For the first life is the way to fulfilment – the other is a dead end.
Help me today, and tomorrow, and for all my future here, to live the ONE life, for which you made me. So that at its end I will know the full harmony of your loving presence freed from the discord of my sin. Amen

*Peter Fox, retired GP and Local Preacher, Tavistock*

*Give thanks for the peace of God which passes all understanding*

# day 18

**In an act of will, O God**, I place myself in your presence. In an act of faith I open myself to your light. In an act of silence, O Lord, I rest in your glory. In an act of love, O Lord, I put myself in your hands.

*Dorothy Kerin, 1889-1963*

**Praying with Christians in Asia (1)**

## Myanmar/Burma
The Methodist Church of Upper Myanmar

*Methodist President:*
C Kapa

*Scholarship students:*
Ngurliana° (in Britain)
San Pwint (in Korea)
Suirengaliana
 (in S Korea)
Van Lala Vena
 (in Taiwan)

**Give thanks** for the enduring faith and growth of **Myanmar** Christians who are suffering under cruel oppression.

**Pray** with Christian leaders who have suffered much hardship; that the door of help and care for the increasing number of those suffering with HIV/AIDS will be opened;

for the work of theological education at Myanmar Theological College, Mandalay, and Tahan Institute of Theology;

for the 17 missionaries and mission field superintendent working in Tahan, Tamu, Letpanchaung and Mindat Districts;

for Lal Rin Sanga (NMA), who is visiting Districts and setting out the priorities of the whole Church.

May God's work of peace, harmony, reconciliation and development continue to be carried out by the Myanmar Council of Churches. May we receive new strength and vision to live out the message of the cross in this 'Golden Land'.

*C Kapa*

## Nepal
The United Mission to Nepal (UMN)

*Director of the UMN:*
Jennie Collins

*Mission Partners:*
ad/n  Paul and Sarah
 Wright,
 Jack and Asha
ad/ad  Michael and
 Maureen
 Hawksworth
t/ed  Allan and
 Andrea Smith

**Give thanks** for a religious people in **Nepal** whose lives revolve around worship, shrines and temples;

for community health teams who offer life-saving hospital treatment to individuals who would otherwise be neglected.

**Pray** with the UMN as it moves towards a policy of greater Nepali participation: that the inspiration of the last 50 years of service will undergird the future;

for the many projects of the UMN, and for strength and safety for its staff and Mission Partners who serve in very complex situations and areas of great risk;

for developing work to face the challenges of HIV/AIDS, peace and reconciliation and the care of women and children;

for exciting opportunities to work with needy communities beyond Kathmandu;

for peace amid growing political instability.

**Give thanks** for the continuing work with survivors of sexual abuse being undertaken from the city centre base.
**Please pray** for our District review: that from it will emerge new ways of working to support and encourage mission locally; for our increasing working together ecumenically.

### Liverpool District

Chair:
James Booth

Secretary:
Ronnie Aitchison

## Apple blossom time – a reflection

It is an old tree, this tree; old before its time, maybe, gnarled and twisted, pushed down by the wind, beaten down by the salt sea spray, cowering behind the dyke.

It is a brave tree, this tree; surviving northerly tempests, southerly storms, easterly floods, westerly gales.

It is a survivor, this tree; gardeners came and went, the garden slid back into peat bog, nothing remained except the tree.

All winter it stands; dark, battered, worn down, lifeless.

*Apple blossom time at Camas*
*Image by Lizz, the gardener*

Yet, with spring, sap rises and the blackened branches burst out in a froth of pink and green.

*Margaret Stewart, Camas, the Iona Centre, Mull*

Lord, we know that nothing can separate us from your love.
In all that this day brings, help me to hold on
to that hope which opens my eyes to the reality of your world
  and yet encourages me;
that hope, which leads me without fear into your future;
that hope, which is your gift in Jesus Christ our Lord,
our Saviour and Friend, in whose name we pray. Amen

*James Booth*

God, make my life an offering to you:
  my worship an offering of my commitment to you;
  my home an offering of my love to you;
  my work an offering of my skill to you;
  my suffering an offering of my pain to you;
  my failure an offering of my need to you;
  my leisure an offering of my relaxation to you;
  my future an offering of my unknown to you.
God, I accept your offering of new life, given to all. Amen

*William Prince, Superintendent Minister*
*of the Redhill and East Grinstead Circuit*

*Give thanks for our share in Christ's ministry of reconciliation*

45

# day 19

**May we, in faith, join in prayer 'without ceasing'** with believers throughout the world, that our prayers may help to bring good changes in the world for our God's sake. May God in Christ bless us richly.

*RPM Tambunan, Indonesia*

Praying with Christians in Asia (2)

## Sri Lanka

*Methodist President:*
Ebenezer Joseph

*Mission Partners:*
th/ad  Rosemary
    Fletcher° and
    James Rowley
lib  Margaret (née
    Julian) and Kithiri
    Mudalige and
    Nathan (+USPG)

*Experience Exchange:*
Helen Morgan

## Indonesia and East Timor

*Gereja Methodista
Bishop:*
R P M Tambunan

*Scholarship student:*
Tumiar Togatorop
    (in Japan)

---

Lord of life and loving God,
who, through your Son, promised life in all its fullness,
we stand speechless in the face of natural calamities
    like the Tsunami.
Surrounded by the dead bodies of thousands of innocent victims, property destroyed and the landscape deformed, we search for words and for your guidance to direct our gaze.
We do not know what to pray, but we do know that 'the Spirit himself intercedes for us with groans that words cannot express'.
We thank you for those who have affirmed life in the midst of death, risking their lives to rescue and help others.
Help us, gracious God, to learn how to be mindful of you and your creation, and save us from greed and exploitation.
Unite the world community in co-ordinated action to do all that we can to prevent such disasters and loss in future.
Reassure us that nothing will be able to separate us from your constant love that is in Christ Jesus our Lord. Amen

*Israel Selvanayagam, South India/UCA*

**Pray** with all who need comfort, healing and hope as they rebuild their homes and communities throughout this region after the devastating effects of the Tsunami;

for the Churches in these countries ministering in this situation and in the continuing need for peace and racial harmony;

for a new constructive relationship between **East Timor and Indonesia** as UN support is withdrawn;

for the Methodist Centennial Celebrations in Indonesia in 2005;

for Jonsen Sembiring (NMA), enabling farmers in Indonesia to use organic methods;

for Dr Ajantha Perara (NMA) who is helping the Church to address the social needs of **Sri Lanka** after more than 20 years of war.

**We give thanks** for the Anglican-Methodist Covenant and growing partnership in mission at all levels of the Church.

**We pray** for the work of the Greater Manchester Churches Together Group and its Development Officer, Graham Kent;

for the new Regional Inter-Faith Forum;

for the work of Monsignor John Devine, representing the faith communities with the Regional Development Agency;

for *Nexus*, a new initiative in mission to the city centre, based at the Central Hall under the leadership of the Revd Cris Acher;

for our Mission Enablers, Dave Martin and Irene Cooper, and our Training and Development Officer, Rosemary Kidd;

for the exciting developments in each of the churches in the Wythenshawe Circuit.

**Manchester and Stockport District**

*Chair:*
Keith Davies

*Secretary:*
Fred Bell

## No easy answers

Creator God, Lord of all things:
we thank you for ever changing skies,
the swell of the sea,
for flowers and lakes, mountains and babies.
But tell us, Lord: where were you on September 11th,
when the twin towers collapsed
and men and women jumped terrified to their deaths?
Where were you when the Tsunami struck
and your gentle sea ran amok,
tearing babies from their mothers' arms?
And what about earthquakes?
Do you make them happen when you're bored?
Forgive us, all powerful God, but we are angry
and desperate as well as grateful and adoring.

Are you, like us, a powerless bystander
at the pain of the world?
Do you weep in your impotence as you uncover bodies
so damaged no one can identify them?
Or is yours the body exhumed from the rubble?
Do you live and suffer and die with us?
Forgive us, O God, for our temerity,
but you made us to question, to argue, to demand answers.
Help us to live with our anger and our pain.
Lord, we believe: help thou our unbelief.

*Sheila Cassidy, a Roman Catholic writer and retired oncologist, Plymouth*

*Give thanks for all who are agents of Christ's compassion*

# day 20

**O Beauty, so ancient and so new!** Late have I loved you though you were always with me. You call to my heart. You burst on my deafness. You scatter my blindness. I draw breath at your fragrance. My heart pants for you. My soul hungers for you. You touch me and I am consumed at the thought of your peace.

*St Augustine, 354-430*

## Praying with Christians in Asia (3)

### Singapore

*Methodist Bishop:*
Robert Solomon

*Mission Partners*
ed  John and Sally
    Barratt

### Malaysia

*Methodist Bishop:*
Hwa Yung

*Special assignment:*
th  David and Rhona
    Burfield

*Scholarship Student:*
Anthony Loke
    (in Britain)

**We pray** for our churches in **Singapore**,
that, as we follow Jesus, 'we may know him more clearly,
love him more dearly and follow him more nearly…'
May each Christian carry the burden of those who are lost,
especially for family members who have yet to receive Jesus
    as Saviour and Lord.
Give us creative ways and boldness to witness
to all who have not heard of Jesus.
May your name be glorified through changed lives,
    a church revived,
    a nation transformed and a world evangelised.

*David Wee, WCBP Singapore/Hull*

**Praise God** for the harmony that is experienced in this multi-racial, multi-faith **Malaysia** and for rapid economic growth.
**Pray** for the Church and its leaders that they may be steadfast in proclaiming the gospel with boldness and wisdom;
for national leaders that they may rule justly and wisely.
May the Holy Spirit anoint and empower each leader with vision and help the churches to steward their resources to benefit the poorer nations around us.

*Hendry and Rita Ponniah WCBP Malaysia/Newcastle*

We pray that when we meet with people of other faiths
we may listen and be enriched by new friendships.
We pray for sensitivity and tolerance;
for understanding and peace in our communities;
for an appreciation of the rich diversity of God's creation.
**Lord, you made us one family: show us how to care.**

**Give thanks** for the opportunities that NE1 (successor to Message and Soul in the City) will provide for mission and service in our region next summer and for the way that churches of every denomination are working together to make this happen.
**Pray** for Rob Hawkins (University Chaplain) and the Ecumenical Team at Newcastle and Northumbria as they minister to staff and students facing uncertainties about their future;
for Ceri Howard, a member of our Ponteland Church, as she becomes Chair of the Methodist Youth Executive.

**Newcastle upon Tyne District**

*Chair:*
Leo Osborn

*Secretary:*
Elizabeth Edwards

*Mission Partners:*
Sipho° and Zime Nyembezi, Nkululeko, Nondumiso, Nosipho and Nokwazi (MCSA) Hendry° and Rita Ponniah, Ian, Ruth, Roy and Tim (Malaysia)

## Song of God

Melodious God,
the song of creation is yours,
vibrant in tone, diverse in harmony,
perfect in pitch and wide in range.
You are the song; we are the singers.

We pray for discernment to interpret this song
when the world sounds flat or out of tune;
for courage to sing out boldly and in unison
to drown the ugly discordant notes of racism,
injustice, poverty and war.

We pray for compassion to listen to the stories
of the poor and oppressed and to the lament
of those who are too heartbroken to sing.

Give us humility not to crave the solo parts
but to rejoice in the music of others.

Most of all we seek the rhythm of your eternal love,
an incarnational song which can be heard as a baby's lullaby.

*Stella Bristow, Oxford Circuit*

Loving God, when we grow weary, undisciplined or unexpectant and cease to pray, help us to see that prayer is not a burden or demand but your precious gift. Remind us of all who pray with us on earth and in heaven and of Jesus Christ our great High Priest, who ever lives to make intercession for us. Then with faith reawakened, hope restored and love renewed, turn us again to share in the ministry of prayer for the salvation of all people, for this is both our calling and your longing. Amen

*Leo Osborn*

*Give thanks for all opportunities to proclaim the gospel*

# day 21

**Help us, O Lord, never to nurse the grievance** that separates us from you and from one another. Grant us grace to forgive those who have wronged us. May we know that no sin is so great that it cannot be confessed; no wound so deep it cannot be healed, and no sinner so lost that grace cannot bring them home.

*William Booth, 1829-1912*

**Praying with Christians** in the Far East (1)

## China

*President of China Christian Council:*
Cao Shengjie

*Amity teachers:*
Michelle Adams
Janet Dickinson
Mick and Anne Kavanagh
Kate Keir
Andrew McLeod
Margaret Scarlett

*Amity is a Chinese non-Government Organisation founded by Christians*

## Hong Kong
(Special Administrative Region of China)

*Methodist President:*
Ralph Lee

*Amity HK:*
Ian Groves

**Give thanks** that the Churches in Hong Kong are able to offer financial support to congregations in mainland China for building churches and for social and educational projects;
for the centrality of the Bible in the life of Chinese Christians (the Amity Printing Company has now produced over 35 million Bibles in different languages and in Chinese Braille);
for a greater openness to religious belief among young people, especially at university.

**Pray** for the Church in China as it seeks to respond to the challenge presented by the increasing numbers of people infected by HIV/AIDS;
for the work of Amity on blindness prevention in 13 provinces, training eye doctors and ophthalmic nurses;
for Amity projects focusing on rural water conservation, AIDS, and teacher training. These are transforming the public image of the Church in China.

**Pray** for the extensive welfare programme in **Hong Kong** – the Methodist Church HK has six multi-purpose social centres meeting many needs;
for the Yang Social Centre's special ministry to abandoned Chinese women and their children;
for the development of peaceful and just relationships between Hong Kong and mainland China – that the motto 'one country, two systems' will work for the benefit of all.

Dear Lord, help our citizens to realise that they will find real peace and meaning only in you, and help the Church to empathise with the needs of the community and the world, that it may be flexible and vibrant enough to serve the needy and to bring justice, truth, peace and hope. Amen

*Katherine Ng, Hong Kong*

### Down District

Superintendent:
Kenneth Todd

Secretary:
Thomas McKnight

**Give thanks** for the fresh focus on dedicated leadership within the churches and for the 'Connexions' training seminars.
**Pray** for evangelism in all the churches that many will find the Saviour;
for the vital commitment of young people within our churches;
for the work of reconciliation within our communities.

### North Lancashire District

Chair:
Stephen Poxon

Secretary:
Andrew Horsfall

Mission Partners:
Garoº and Dada Kilagi, Geua, Gima and Elijah (Papua New Guinea)

**Give thanks** for those churches responding to the opportunities within their midst with fresh ways of worship and mission;
for the growth at Whalley and their daily 7.00am prayer meeting;
for innovative work with young people at Knott End through the 'Dream Scheme'.
**Pray** for the Blackburn Diocese and our joint commitment to a five-point Covenant for Mission and for the URC whose realigned boundaries are now co-terminus with the District and Diocese;
for our growing partnerships with the Church in Sierra Leone, Papua New Guinea, our WCBP family newly arrived among us and Uruguay;
for the work team's visit to Sierra Leone and the sharing of experience.

### Tease me to go deeper

my good Lord, slain and risen One,
rashly and childlike I ask you that,
as you engaged in conversation
with the important Nicodemus
who came to you by night,
and the insignificant Samaritan woman
whom you approached at midday,
so you will draw me into conversation…
Tease me out of getting stuck
in my certainties about who you ought to be.
Tease me to go deeper, to the source,
rather than fussing about buckets and drink.
Confront me in my shadow self,
    my denials, my timidity,
until I come to know that, in you,
    I AM is speaking to me. Amen
*Based on John 3.1-21 and 4.1-42*

*Thomas Cullinan,*
*a Catholic Benedictine monk, living near Liverpool*

*Give thanks for the presence and power of the Holy Spirit*

# day 22

**Let me prefer your presence**, O God, to all other company. Let me exalt your name, O Lord, above all other names and let me love your will, O God, beyond all other desires; for the sake of Jesus Christ. Amen

*Therèse of Lisieux, 1873-1897*

 **Praying with Christians** in the Far East (2)

---

## Japan

*General Secretary of the Kyodan, the United Church of Christ in Japan:*
Shiro Harada

*Mission Partners:*
ed   Michael and
     Svetlana Armstrong
     (+CA)
ed   Sheila Norris
ed   Daniel and Yasuko
     Dellming, Momoko
     and Daisuke

## Korea

*Presiding Bishop:*
Kwang Young

**Pray** for Christians in **Japan** (less than 1%) witnessing in a predominantly Shinto and Buddhist culture;
for those committed to working in schools and colleges – that their quiet influence may be of lasting value;
for those whose lives are still affected by nuclear contamination;
for reconciliation between North and South **Korea**;
for Koreans living in Britain and worshipping in our churches.

Eternal God,
we say good morning to you.
Hallowed be your name.
Early in the morning, before we begin our work,
we praise your glory.
Renew our bodies as fresh as the morning flowers.
Open our inner eyes, as the sun casts new light
upon the darkness
which prevailed over the night.
Deliver us from all captivity...
Restore justice and freedom,
as a mighty stream running continuously
as day follows day.
We thank you for the gift of this morning,
and a new day to work with you. Amen

*Masao Takenaka, Japan (Christian Conference of Asia)*

Come now, O Prince of Peace, make us as one body.
Come, O Lord Jesus, reconcile your people.
Come now, God of love, make us one body.
Come now and set us free, O God, our Saviour.
Come, hope of Unity, make us one body.
Come, O Lord Jesus, and reconcile all nations.

*Lee Geonyong, Korea*
*From USPG Prayer Diary May/August 2004*

**Give thanks** for the 'Athenaeum' Cybercafe in Melbourne (Castle Donington Circuit), open five days a week: for the vision of those who established it and their determination to employ a full-time worker to make it more a part of the community.

**Pray** for South Derbyshire Circuit where the West Street Church in Swadlincote has entered into a partnership which will be the basis of a new community development scheme renewing buildings and leading to a close working relationship with other denominations in an ecumenical area;

for our children, young people and young adults, that we may discover new and right ways to encourage them to feel part of each other and part of the Church of Christ.

### Nottingham and Derby District

*Chair:*
Wesley Blakey

*Secretary:*
Helen Watson

Disabling darkness of the night
magnifies aches and tortures thought;
disarms sense,
increases fears,
reduces comfort into nought.

But comes the dawn and warming light
and all the horrors melt away.
Faith returns –
and confidence
that God is in this glorious day.

For Resurrection lives in me;
I rise – assured by holy sight.
All darkness
is impermanent,
defeated by eternal light.

*Wesley Blakey*

Holy One, Living One, Comforting One,
God of many names,
Source of All, Word of Wisdom, Revealer of Truth,
you alone are worthy of our praise and thanksgiving.
Give to us such knowledge,
awe and wonder of yourself
that our lives may give you honour
in both worship and service,
through Jesus Christ our Lord. Amen

*Andy Lyons, student at Queen's College, Birmingham*

*Give thanks for the ministry of the word, the sacraments and prayer*

# day 23

**We bless you, O God,** for the love that never fails; we thank you for the blood that cleanses from all sin; we praise you for the pardon that sets the sinner free and we glorify you for the gift of eternal life in your Son, our Saviour Jesus Christ. Amen

*Martyn Lloyd-Jones, 1899-1981*

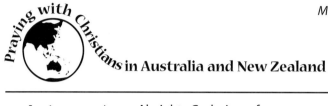 in Australia and New Zealand

---

### Aotearoa/ New Zealand

*Methodist President:*
Lynne Frith

### The Uniting Church of Australia
(UCA)

*President:*
Dean Drayton

Almighty God, giver of grace
Creator, Redeemer and Spirit.
We are your people
of scalding earth and dust,
of lake and forest.

Work through your people
to bless the world
with blessing of water, bread and wine,
the blessing of speech and silence,
the blessing of skill and art,
the blessing of prayer
and loving service.
Work through your people
to love and challenge the world,
to pursue peace and demand integrity,
to speak for the voiceless,
'to walk on the side of wounded humanity,
to follow Christ
even when the way points to a cross'.
Together your people say, Amen

*St Paul's Parish Prayer (Presbyterian/Methodist) Taupo, New Zealand*

Loving God, we thank you that our minds are expanded to see the many ways you act and bless as we hear the stories of how you work in other lives.
God of diversity, you delight in the variety of your creation; help us to receive the differences of others as your gift.
Thank you that, in Christ, people of all lands and cultures are one through our shared relationship with you.
Give us courage to embrace the vision of a multicultural Church.

*Terence Corkin, General Secretary of the Uniting Church in Australia*

**Give thanks** for exciting possibilities which will arise when Buckinghamshire helps us to create a new District;
for the willingness to embrace different ideas, and grasp new opportunities for ministry and mission.
**Pray** for all people affected by the forthcoming boundary changes and those involved in ongoing discussions;
for sensitivity and understanding;
for a sharing of ideas and a good use of resources;
for an openness to listen to one another's concerns.

## Persecution

*We pray for the* **Keston Institute, Oxford**
*which works with Christians who are persecuted for their faith in other parts of the world.*
Loving God,
we pray with all who suffer persecution
and discrimination because of their faith,
that we may stand together in times of fear and uncertainty
and live in solidarity one with another.
Strengthen us as we seek to follow your Son, Jesus Christ,
to carry the cross in a hostile society.
Give to us all courage in the face of ridicule,
strength to go on loving
and hope in the coming of your Kingdom. Amen

> 'Real intercession is not merely a petition but involves costly surrender to God for the work God wants done...'
> *Adapted from Evelyn Underhill*

Dear Lord,
you are the hope of all the earth: we worship you.
You are the centre and circumference of our life:
    we abide in you.
We thank you for Jesus, the baby in the cradle,
the man upon the cross, the body in the tomb
and the King upon the throne.
Help your Church to reveal Christ's face in the world,
and to be the loving touch of Christ upon the world. Amen
*Ken Todd, Down District, Ireland*

### Oxford and Leicester District

*Chair:*
Alison Tomlin

*Secretary:*
Martin Wellings

*Mission Partners:*
Edward° and Esther Sakwe, Electa, Lucella, Masoma and Jemea (Cameroon)
Asif° and Rohama° Karam, Zarah, Zoya and Zeenia (Pakistan)

*Give thanks for our baptism and our call to serve Christ*

# day 24

**Flood my soul, O God**, with your presence. Penetrate my whole being with your Spirit. Shine through me with your light. May others look into my life and see only their Lord and Saviour, Jesus Christ. Amen

*John Henry Newman, 1801-1890*

 **in the Pacific (1)**

---

**Pacific Conference of Churches (PCC)**

*General Secretary:*
Valamotu Palu

**United Church in Papua New Guinea**

*Moderator:*
Samson Lowa

**United Church of the Solomon Islands**

*Moderator:*
Philemon Riti

ed/n    Richard and Katherine Jackson

Liberator God,
who comes to the oppressed of every time and place,
we pray for the peoples of the Pacific
seeking development and change
but wanting to hold on to the best of traditional values:
to respect the sacredness of land, sea and air,
and all that ties them together in community.
We pray with the Pacific Council of Churches
for all who feel called to be prophets:
to step out and risk unpopularity,
to oppose corruption and stand by the truth.
**Lord, you made us one family: show us how to care.**

**We give thanks** for the example and challenge of unity in these two United Churches.
**We pray** for all ministering to the growing number of people infected by HIV/AIDS, remembering that the Churches provide a large proportion of health care in these nations;
for women learning new skills and seeking a better quality of life;
for the future of **Papua New Guinea** as its people celebrate 30 years of Independence;
for the continuing witness of the Helen Goldie Hospital in the **Solomon Islands**.

## A Pacific islander's prayer

O Jesus,
be the canoe that holds me up in the sea of life;
be the rudder that keeps me on the straight road;
be the outrigger that supports me in times of temptation.
Let your Spirit be my sail that carries me through each day.
Keep my body strong, so I can paddle steadfastly on
    in the voyage of life.

**We give thanks** for the developing link between our District and the Villa Cont do Pinhal Methodist Church, Sao Paulo in Brazil.
**We pray** that the group who visited Brazil will be able to share their experience across the District, broaden our horizons and encourage our involvement in the World Church.
**We pray** for the District Partnership Programme: with Brazil, with our ecumenical sisters and brothers and neighbouring circuits, as we respond to the challenge of twenty-first- century mission by sharing resources, ideas and mutual encouragement;
for fresh expressions of church:

> exciting Cell Church and youth workers in rural areas,
> outreach in Stonehouse and Keyham at Plymouth,
> plans for ecumenical work in new housing developments
> encouraging the discovery of local gifts to pastor each
> church and support the decreasing number of ministers.

### Plymouth and Exeter District

*Chair:*
John Carne

*Secretary:*
Linda Barriball

*Brazil exchange visit*

## Travelling companions

God our companion, we are together on a journey.
You are always there guiding us towards the right path.
Help us not to stray onto meandering roads of misconceptions,
even when it feels as if we are on a ring road going round
in unending circles...
Help us choose the right way:
the pathway of love and caring for others:
the way of helping those less fortunate than ourselves;
the way of Christ which refuses to take others for granted.

God our creator, on this journey you call us
to 'tread softly' on your earth.
Give us hope and gentleness that we may learn
to live in peace and harmony within your beautiful creation
which our greed has spoiled.
Lord, transform your world, our relationships and our lives.

Lord, in this time of silence let us reflect on our journey of life
and maybe reconsider the paths we are taking.
Be our companion as we journey on. Amen

*Kevin Jones, MAYC President*

Listening God, tune our ears to hear your voice amid the clamour of our busy lives. May our living be the acting out of our praying in word and deed. Amen

*John Carne*

*Give thanks for our part in the mission of Christ to the world*

# day 25

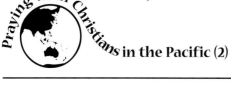

in the Pacific (2)

**Begotten of your love, O Father**, we are made in your image. Cared for all our days, we are never beyond your sight. Enfolded in your heart, we are never out of your thought. To think of you is rest. To know you is eternal life. To see you is the end of all desire. To serve you is perfect freedom. To love you is everlasting joy. Amen

*W E Orchard, 1877-1955*

## Tonga

*Methodist President:*
'Alifalete Mone

*Mission Partner:*
sp/ad  David and
   Val May
ed  Ruth Watt

*Scholarship Student:*
Henry Niumeitolu°
   (Tonga)

## Samoa

*Acting President:*
Siatua Leulua 'iali'i

*Scholarship Student:*
Mosese Mailo-
   Fuaiva'a

## Fiji

*Methodist President:*
Laisiasa Ratabacaca

*Mission Partner:*
th   David Upp°

**Give thanks** that many Christians in each of these nations meet daily in their villages for prayer and continue to keep Sunday as a day for worship and family life.

**Pray** for young people being drawn from traditional ways by the influences of the developed world;

for those who work with them in schools and camps to increase their awareness of the dangers of drugs, alcohol and HIV/AIDS;

for Theological Colleges seeking to develop a theology which reflects traditional beliefs and customs;

for those who seek justice, integrity and racial harmony even when it means standing out from the crowd;

for Lotafaga Lima (NMA), leading seminars and workshops to encourage church members in **Samoa** to share the gospel.

## Global warming

Eternal God, Creator of the heavens and the earth,
we are part of your world and not exempt from its problems.
The very low-lying islands, in this vast ocean of the Pacific,
cry out to the powerful nations of the earth
to save them from the destructive force of rising sea levels.
Almighty God, may our voices be heard in the World Summit
concerning climate change.

*Sina Vaipuna, Tonga*

 ## Prayer from Hawaii

Father of all humankind, make the roof of my house
   wide enough for all opinions;
oil the door of my house so that it opens easily
   to friend and stranger;
and set such a table in my house that my whole family
   may speak kindly and freely around it.

*Source unknown*

**Give thanks** for ways in which God works through people, transforming individuals and the community.
**Pray** for the vulnerable, especially older people and those who are disabled;
for those who think they have little need of God and feel the Church is irrelevant.

### Portadown District

*Superintendent:*
Maurice Laverty

*Secretary:*
Brian Sweeney

---

**Thank God** for the commitment to prayer evidenced in the annual publication of the Sheffield District Prayer Handbook (also available on www.sheffieldmethodist.org)
Thank God that the Roman Catholic Bishop of Hallam, the Anglican Bishop of Sheffield and our Chair of District meet together in each other's homes for a monthly prayer breakfast.
**Pray** for the many asylum seekers who worship with us, enrich our lives and who pray each day that they will be given leave to stay in our land;
for the housebound who, unable to be as active in church life as they once were, now exercise a vital prayer ministry often in the long watches of the night.

### Sheffield District

*Chair:*
Vernon Marsh

*Secretary:*
Gillian Newton

*Mission Partners:*
Jonathan° and Elizabeth Gichaara, Neene, Israel and Muthomi (Kenya)

## Resisting Temptation

In those confines of our lives
which we closely guard...
where we allow no mortal to penetrate
except our own selves...
may the Holy Spirit illumine with the light of God.

In those areas of our hearts
where we harbour hatred, racial bias and discord;
those areas... those deep recesses of our lives
which are filled with 'I am better than thou...'
may the light of Christ shine.

In those times and places
when and where we see poverty and squalor
and we have the power to change the situation,
may God help us to resist the temptation to look the other way,
and give us the grace to apply ourselves... as agents of change.

*Jonathan Gichaara, Kenya/World Church Tutor,*
*Urban Theology Unit, Sheffield*

*Give thanks for unity, God's will and gift to the Church*

# Europe

*Secretary for Europe:*
Colin Ride

> To clasp the hands in prayer
> is the beginning of an uprising
> against the disorder of the world.
>
> *Karl Barth*

*Mural on UMC Prison Chapel
Ekaterinburg, Russia*

# Ireland

Al = **Albania**
Au = **Austria**
B  = **Belgium**
Bo = **Bosnia-Herzegovina**
Cr = **Croatia**
Cz = **Czech Republic**
E  = **Estonia**
G  = **Gibraltar**
Gr = **Greece**
H  = **Hungary**
L  = **Latvia**
Li = **Lithuania**
Lu = **Luxembourg**
M  = **Moldavia**
Mc = **Macedonia**
Mn = **Montenegro**
Sb = **Serbia**
Sl = **Slovak Republic**
Sn = **Slovenia**
Sw = **Switzerland**

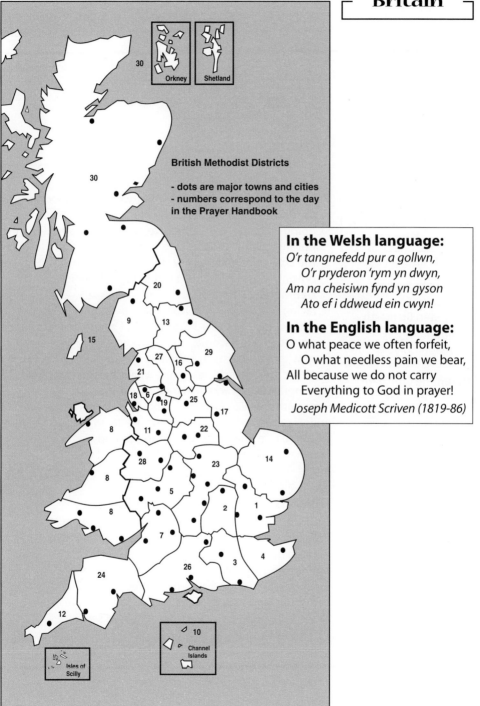

**British Methodist Districts**

- dots are major towns and cities
- numbers correspond to the day
  in the Prayer Handbook

Orkney

Shetland

**In the Welsh language:**
*O'r tangnefedd pur a gollwn,*
*O'r pryderon 'rym yn dwyn,*
*Am na cheisiwn fynd yn gyson*
*Ato ef i ddweud ein cwyn!*

**In the English language:**
O what peace we often forfeit,
O what needless pain we bear,
All because we do not carry
Everything to God in prayer!
*Joseph Medicott Scriven (1819-86)*

Isles of
Scilly

Channel
Islands

# day 26

**Guide your Church, O Lord**, with your perpetual providence; that it may walk warily in times of quiet, and boldly in times of trouble; through Jesus Christ our Lord. Amen

*Franciscan Breviary*

 Praying with Christians in Europe (1)

---

## The United Methodist Northern Europe Central Conference

*Bishop:* Öystein Olsen

*Superintendents:*

**Norway:** Ola Westad, Vidar Sten Bjerkseth

**Sweden:** Anders Svensson, Solveig Högberg, Bimbi Ollberg

**Denmark:** Christian Alsted, Finn Uth

**Finland** *(Swedish language)* Tom Hellsten, Fredrik Wegelius

**Finland** *(Finnish language)* Timo Virtanen

**Estonia:** Taavi Hollman

**Latvia:** Arijs Viksna

**Lithuania:** Chet Cataldo

**Russia:** *Bishop of the UMC in Eurasia:* Hans Vaxby

*Mission Partner:* p Nicola Vidamour°

*Scholarship Student:* Ilya Kovalev (in Britain)

**The Conference of European Churches**
*General Secretary:*
Keith Clements,
Collin Williams

**Give thanks** for faithfulness and hope.

**Pray** with Churches in this region who are exploring new ways of ministry, taking risks and reaching out:

- doing without a headquarters' office in **Sweden** and putting their resources into local congregations to meet the challenge to be 'a new church for our time';
- putting non-Christians at the top of their agenda in **Denmark**;
- facing the challenge to train more personnel in Finland;
- witnessing against a backgound of social and economic uncertainty in **Estonia**.

**Pray** with Methodists in Lithuania giving thanks that for the first time this Church has sent a Volunteers Mission Team to Kaliningrad, Russia and held medical clinics;

**Pray** with families in Russia who were bereaved, wounded and traumatised in the horrific siege in Beslan as they continue to come to terms with this tragedy;

for small Bible study groups and congregations.

## HIV/AIDS – a challenge from Russia:

*'The world has already failed Africa: will it fail us?'*

**Pray** with people with HIV/AIDS who are fearful and in despair, isolated by their family and community
but needing love and hope...
for counselling and treatment centres
and for all who seek to make young people more aware
of the dangers of casual and unprotected sex;
that those who are infected may be more open about their illness
and that fear and stigma may be replaced by love and acceptance;
for elderly grandparents grieving the loss of sons and daughters
and now bringing up their orphaned grandchildren...
**Lord, you made us one family: show us how to care.**

**Give thanks** for churches and groups that are discovering new ways of 'being church' in their corporate life together;
for developing ecumenical relationships at all levels;
for tangible signs of growth in new members, local preachers and worship leaders.

**Pray** for the District in this year of transition and change;
for the staff team covering for Tom Stuckey's absence during his year as President of the Conference;
for staff and residents of Methodist Homes at Maidment Court (Poole) and Greenways (Bognor Regis).

### Southampton District

*Acting Chair:*
Robert McBain

*Secretary:*
Lesley Martin

## A parent's sacrifice

Generous God, my daughter responded to an invitation,
   in your name, to journey to Russia.
This fills me with pride at her deep faith,
   boundless courage and linguistic skill.
Yet, her absence, Lord, is a thief to my joy.
I am wrapped in moments of emptiness
   as I miss her laughter, visits and shared outings.

Her journey has a purpose.
   Fill her with an attitude of mission.
   Fill me with gentleness of spirit.

Her journey has obstacles.
   Fill her with strength and patience for each crisis.
   Fill me with grace to support her in the struggle.

She journeys with the greatest friend of all.
   Fill all families separated by barriers of distance
   with your calming, constant presence in our lives. Amen

*Mollie Priest, mother of Nicola Vidamour, Mission Partner in Russia*

*Nicola Vidamour (right) and Nelli Mamonova, Superintendent (left)*

Father and Mother God,
enfold us with your gracious presence
so that our praying and living become one.
Jesus, Son of God, as living witnesses,
help us to speak with confidence
and in ways which make sense to people outside the Church.
Holy Spirit of God, as your obedient people,
enable us to see your activity in the world
and inspire us to join with you in that work. Amen

*Tom Stuckey*

*Give thanks for the suffering and victory of Jesus Christ*

# day 27

**Eternal Light, shine into our hearts**. Eternal Goodness, deliver us from evil. Eternal Power, be our support. Eternal Wisdom, scatter our darkness. Eternal Pity, have mercy on us, that with all our mind, soul and strength we may seek your face and finally by your mercy be brought to everlasting life; through Christ our Lord. Amen

*Alcuin of York, c. 732-804*

**Praying with Christians in Europe (2)**

---

## Belgium

*President of the Eglise Protestante Unie:*
Daniel Vanescote

## The United Methodist German Central Conference

*Bishop:*
Rosemarie Wenner

*Mission Partners:*
p Colin° and Muriel Barrett
p Barry° and Gillian Sloan, Michael and Megan
p Vanessa Cook

**Give thanks** for leaders of vision and hope.
**Pray** with those who are leading revitalisation initiatives that the Church may begin to move forward;
with small churches which need help and encouragement to revive their work and mission;
with all who are engaged in dialogue between people of different faiths to build tolerance and understanding;
for all who have turned away from the Church;
for the development of a new spirit of reconciliation between East and West.

As the United Methodist Church in **Germany**, we are thankful for every opportunity to fulfil our mission. We celebrate the fact that more churches are now reaching out to the poor and seeking to live alongside them.
We pray for all who suffer under the constraints of our new economic system, especially for those who have lost their jobs, or who fear unemployment;
for young people that they may see a future for their lives and for older people that they will not lose hope.

*Walter Klaiber*

God is our Creator:
**and we live in the freedom of being God's sons and daughters.**

God is the Love which is our foundation and light of our lives:
**and we want to live in mutual confidence.**

God is the Peace which exceeds every imagination:
**and we want to live in peace with each other.**

God is the healing touch which gives rest to all who are weary and are carrying heavy burdens:
**and we want to be a healed and healing community. Amen**

*Conference of European Churches 12th Assembly, 2003*

In this Year of Prayer **we give thanks** for a quarter of a century publishing prayers under the WYS Book logo here in West Yorkshire.

**We pray** for the work of our new Mission Enabling Officer, the Revd Nick Blundell and the Mission Enabling Team drawn from around our District as they begin work together;

for guidance and courage as in circuits and churches we search for Fresh Expressions of mission and ministry relevant to this place and our time.

## West Yorkshire District

*Chair:*
Peter Whittaker

*Secretary:*
Ruth Gee

## Calls you one and calls you all...

Creator God, you have called us to do your will in the world,
in the name of Jesus.
You have called us to be
shop assistants and social workers
truckers and teachers
carpenters and chemists
engineers and evangelists
labourers and lawyers
and much else besides.

We pray with all people in their daily life and work:
enjoying fulfilment in a purposeful job or challenging vocation,
staring at the uncertainty of redundancy or dismissal,
holding immense responsibility and facing testing decisions,
feeling exploited by injustice in trade,
caring for others, unpaid and unsung.

And we pray with people for whom time passes slowly:
seeking employment, frustrated by repeated refusals,
unable to work through illness and incapacity,
retired, now wondering where they are still wanted,
finding their work a drudge, dreading each new day,
still listening for God's call.

Enabling God,
we commit the insight of our minds,
the labour of our hands
and the love of our hearts,
as we share in daily community life
and shape the future of your created world. Amen

*John A Bell, Vice President of the Methodist Conference*

*Give thanks for the power of Christ to transform our suffering*

# day 28

**Grant me grace, O God**, to take your Son for my Redeemer; his life for my example, his word for my rule, his Spirit for my guide, his wounds for my healing and his cross for my salvation, that he may take possession of my heart, now and for ever. Amen

*Jeremy Taylor, 1613-1657*

## Praying with Christians in Central Europe (1)

---

### United Methodist Central and Southern Europe Central Conference

*Bishop:* Heinrich Bolleter

*Superintendents:*

**Algeria**
Daniel Nussbaumer

**Austria:** Lothar Poell

**Bulgaria:** Bedros Altunian

*Mission Partners:*
sd Peter and Samantha
  Taylor and Rosanna

*Scholarship Student:*
Mihail Stefanov° (in Britain)

**Czech Republic**
Josef Cervenak

**Georgia**
*Scholarship Student:*
Irina Ramishvili

**Slovak Republic**
Pavel Prochazka

**Hungary:** Istvan Csernak

**Poland:** Edward Puslecki

**Switzerland/France**
Daniel Nussbaumer
Markus Bach
Hanna, Elsi Atorfer and
  Walter Wilhelm

**Give thanks** for the vision and activity of the United Methodist Conference covering 22 countries, wanting to influence the new Europe so that it is seen as a new community growing out of the traditions of faith;

for the considerable work being done throughout Europe among migrants and ethnic minorities;

for Chinese work in Graz, **Austria**:

> *Fifteen years ago a Swiss couple, trying to find a Methodist Church in Graz, stopped a young Chinese man to ask the way. He said he had never heard of such a thing as 'church', so they invited him to go along with them. He was baptised four months later and has since brought many other Chinese restaurant owners with him.*

**Pray** for the Methodist Church in Varna, Bulgaria, opened in 2003. The original church had been converted into a puppet theatre by the Communists. It is now a social centre serving the needs of the town;

for Kalas Demirdjian (NMA) serving with three Armenian congregations in Bulgaria and working with young people and immigrant families;

for work with the gypsy congregation in Alsoozsolca, **Hungary**, helping them to apply for jobs amid high unemployment;

for Sergey and Esther Bogomazuik (NMAs) in the **Carpathian Ukraine**, opening up new work with young people.

Remembering the evil and suffering of Auschwitz, may we have the strength not to remain silent in the face of any evil that dehumanises another individual, ethnic group or nation.

**Give thanks** for the growing number of ministers from different parts of the world who have come to serve in the District and who bring challenge and freshness of approach; for the opening of a new church at Wellington, and for circuits imaginatively facing tough decisions about their future.

**Pray** for the new Chair as he brings leadership to the District and works with District officers to support the circuits; for the newly appointed District Mission Enabler.

### Lord, you are there

Lord of wonder and joy, who shares our excitement,
hears the shriek of laughter, sees the smile of delight,
you celebrate life with us.
    In our happiness we know you are there.

Lord of suffering and pain, who shares the hurt within,
hears the heartfelt cry, sees the tears of frustration,
you cradle us in silence.
    In our distress we know you are there.

Lord of truth and grace, sinless One, who shares our
        human nature,
hears our frequently rehearsed excuses, sees the frown
        of self-doubt,
your saving power is timeless.
    In our weakness we know you are there.

Lord of hope and freedom, who shares our yearning
        for all things made new,
hears the elation in a dream become reality, sees our glimpse
        of a new dawn,
you are key to everyone's dreams.
    In our longing we know you are there.

*Eddie Newton, Local Preacher, Redhill*

---

**Wolverhampton and Shrewsbury District**

*Chair:*
John Howard

*Secretary:*
Brenda Shuttleworth

*Mission Partners:*
Solomonaº and Ana Potogi, Lusa and Wesley (Samoa)
Danielº and Laura Williams, Danny, Debbie and Damaris (Cuba)

---

24-hour God,
always and everywhere,
may your Holy Name be praised.
Always and everywhere
may your people raise their voices.
Always and everywhere
may your Kingdom come, your will be done. Amen

*Peter Whittaker*

*Give thanks for signs of renewal in the Church through the Holy Spirit*

# day 29

**Come, Holy Spirit, come as the fire of love** to enkindle us. Come as Lord and Giver of Life to dwell within us. Come as the Sevenfold Gift to renew us. Come as the rushing wind to drive us forward. Come as the holy Dove to launch us heavenward. Come as the Wellspring to purify our souls. Amen

*Christina Rossetti, 1830-1894*

Praying with Christians in Central Europe (2)

---

**United Methodist Central and Southern Europe Central Conference** (continued)

**Serbia and Montenegro**
*Superintendent:*
Ana Palik-Kuncak

**Macedonia**
*Superintendent:*
Wilhelm Nausner

**Give thanks** for vision and commitment; for the ecumenical Council in Macedonia, which includes Orthodox and Muslim leaders.

**Pray** with Churches witnessing under serious political and economic pressures and for the whole Balkan region whose future is uncertain;

for the significant ministry among Roma people driven out of Kosovo, giving thanks for the hope and joy inspired by the opening of a new church home in Kochani, **Macedonia**, and by the Church Youth Camp where, for the first time, Roma young people felt they had been treated as human beings;

for Katarina Nikolic's work (NMA) among the Roma people in Srbobran, **Serbia**;

for Mirce Tancev (NMA) giving pastoral care, preaching and working with young people in Monospitovo, Macedonia;

for Gordana Miteva (NMA), leader of the Miss Stone Centre, responding to the needs of the Strumica community.

---

### Breakthrough

When all around you is emptiness,
when all you can hear is silence,
when all you can see are walls,
when everybody is deaf to your cries,
and everybody is blind to your tears –

Then you must see the world as children do:
with bright eyes and lovely smile,
with heart full of love and joy,
with faith and hope big as a mountain.

This is the way to escape your own prison
and the way to reach the Kingdom of God.

*Tinka Krsteva, Strumica, Macedonia*

**Give thanks** for ongoing ecumenical opportunities especially building on the covenant relationship with the Diocese of York.
**Pray** for a growing understanding between our partner Churches and our District – where relationships are easy and where they are more challenging;
for rural communities who are striving to discern how to maintain an effective Christian presence.

### York and Hull District

*Chair:*
Stephen Burgess

*Secretary:*
Rosemary Harrison

*Mission Partners:*
David° and Jessie Wee (Singapore)

## Peace

Lord, in a world torn apart by greed and selfishness...
in a heart tossed on waves of uncertainty,
you offer peace –
    not of monetary gain or problems halved,
    but peace that reaches into the very source of life
    speaks new meaning, transforms, renews.

Lord, in a life that has no hope, from which all love has fled,
you offer peace –
    not fashioned to ear and eye, to cheque book,
    pension, credit rate,
    but your free gift of grace,
    reaching into the world, heart by Son-drenched heart.

*Adapted from a prayer, based on John 14.27,*
*by Patricia Batstone, Honiton*

Creative God,
who spoke the world into being,
create new life, new hope in your people.

Redemptive God,
who embraced the world with your love in Jesus,
enfold each one of us in your grace.

Sustaining God,
who, by your Spirit, holds together the universe
strengthen us, your Church, by your presence.

As we worship and serve you
help us to walk the way of Jesus
this day and all our days. Amen

*David L Jones, Deputy Chair of York and Hull*

*Give thanks for God's faithful departed servants who have revealed his grace and enriched our Christian pilgrimage*

# day 30

**With the angels and saints**, each day and each night, each shade and each light, I bend my knee in the eye of the Father who created me, in the eye of the Son who redeemed me, in the eye of the Spirit who cleansed me. In love and affection, in wisdom and grace, in love and in fear, for ever and ever. Amen

*Gaelic Prayer to the Trinity*

## Praying with Christians in Southern Europe

### Portugal

*Bishop:*
Sifredo Teixeira
rt   Cora Aspey

### Spain
### Iglesia Evangelica Española

*President:*
Joel Cortès

### Italy

*Methodist President:*
Massimo Aquilante

*Mission Partners:*
p Augusto° and Mirna Giron, Gabriel and Debora

**Give thanks** for commitment and risk in taking social action.
**Pray** with those in **Portugal** who want to move from being a Church in which the clergy are seen to be active to one where all use their gifts. This is a minority Church within a largely Roman Catholic country. It has few ministers, but walks in faith. Pray for its ministry among immigrants and for Ana Aco Martins (NMA) who is working with immigrants in Moita; for the John Wesley Centre in Braga and the Social Centre in Monte Pedral offering day care to children.
Pray for mission and social outreach in **Spain**, especially among migrant people and among those who come to Spain to retire with no network of social relationships;
for Pastor George Ennin (NMA) working among African immigrants in Northern **Italy**;
for Evelyn Aghom (NMA) Reception Officer for the Pelligrino della Terra Project which is helping women who are victims of the sex trade in Italy.

May God bless you with discomfort at easy answers,
half truths, and superficial relationships,
so that you may live deep within your heart.

May God bless you with anger at injustice…
so that you may work for justice, freedom and peace.

May God bless you with tears to shed
for those who suffer from pain…
so that you may reach out your hand
to comfort them and to turn their pain into joy.

And may God bless you with enough foolishness
to believe that you can make a difference in this world,
so that you can do what others claim cannot be done. Amen

*From a Franciscan Blessing (source unknown)*

**Give thanks** for a strong and growing commitment to trade justice and AIDS Awareness and the response to the gifts and the needs of the World Church.

**Pray** for leadership teams, in geographically large circuits, finding new ways to support and encourage congregations;

for the Northern Region Group preparing for the 2006 Conference in Edinburgh – the first one to be held in Scotland;

for newly appointed people to resource Safeguarding and ministry formation in the particular context of Scotland.

**Scotland District**

*Chair:*
James Jones

*Secretary:*
Janet Murray

---

**Give thanks** for opportunities to lead assemblies in schools and worship in residential homes.

**Pray** for local preachers and officers of the District as they share with the staff in encouraging worship and mission;

for guidance as the District makes plans for its mission in the future with trimmed resources.

**Shetland District**

*Chair:*
Jeremy Dare

*Secretary:*
Sylvia White

Almighty God,
we are honoured, blessed and saved through your costly, loving commitment to us in Jesus Christ our Lord. We place our hands in yours, praying for the courage to travel where you lead, observe as you see and respond with the grace of your holy love. Amen

*Jeremy Dare*

Loving Father,
thank you for the privilege of being your family.
We praise you for your love revealed to us,
and we trust your promises.
Your love is never withdrawn –
even when we are disobedient and unloving.
Inspire us to live as your children,
obeying your commandments,
loving one another in practical ways.
May those who do not recognise your love, turn to you.
We pray in the name of Jesus Christ, our Saviour. Amen

*Constance Magnus, Jamaica*

*Give thanks for our foretaste of the life of the world to come*

**We commend to you, O Lord**, our souls and our bodies; our prayers and our hopes; our health and our work; our life and our death; our families and our friends; our neighbours and our fellow men and women, this day and always. Amen

*Lancelot Andrewes, 1555-1626*

Praying with the oikoumene World Council of Churches

*Mission Partners and others recently returned from overseas:*

Ros Colwill (Nigeria)
Peter and Sarah Dockree (Nigeria)
David Duffield (Sierra Leone)
David (RIP) and Keiko Gray (Japan)
Else Iverson (Kenya)
Carolyn Lawrance (Zambia)
Paul and Rachel Lindoewood (Kenya)
Jodi and Michelle Marshall (China)
Paul McMaster (Kenya)
David and Sue Palmer (Sri Lanka)
Rebecca Pennells (Zambia)
Jane Petty (Zambia)
Adam Richards (St Vincent)
Liz Rose (Benin)
David and Mary Sarson (Kenya)
Matthew Siddall (China)
Andrew and Rosemary Symonds (Bangladesh)
Paul and Mary Thomas (Jamaica)
John Wall (Zambia)
Jo White (China)
Andrew and Caroline Wickens (Kenya)
John and Jenny Willetts (PNG)
Rosanna Woodruff (Ghana)

## Decade to Overcome Violence (2001-2010)

Loving God, may we be more open to the leading of your Spirit and the vision of the WCC, so that we may come together as your people. Deepen our commitment to unity and to facing the issues that divide the world. Transform us into a reconciling presence in your divided world. In the name of him who prayed that we may be one, your Son, Jesus Christ. Amen

Do everything in common:
unite in one prayer, one petition,
one mind, one hope,
in love and faultless joy.
All this in Jesus Christ and there is nothing better than he.
So make haste, all of you,
to come together as one temple of God around the altar,
around the one Jesus Christ,
who came forth from the one Father,
while still remaining one with him
and has returned to unity with him.

*St Ignatius of Antioch (c.35 – c.107)*

God of the land, we hunger and thirst for redemption,
knowing that it is we who must change
in order for your Kingdom to come on earth.
Send us out of this church and into your world;
out of our slumber and into life;
out of our apathy and into action;
out of our own unsatisfied hunger for riches
and into the world, to celebrate together the harvest
you give us to share. Amen

*Kevin Fray, Methodist Relief and Development Fund*

# Feeding the multitude

*A reflection on a Family Fun Day at Redhill,*
*based on Mark 6.34-44 and John 21.15-17*

*Mission Partners in*
*transit or in training:*

Stephen and Lorraine
Emery-Wright
Mark and Elizabeth
Leeming
Helen Moorehead
Kathryn Thomas
Marlene Wilkinson

It came to pass that one day a small group of church members began looking at the community around them to enter into their situation and pray for them. And God said to the church, 'Feed my sheep.'

'But Social Services can do this better than we can,' said the church people. 'They have degrees in Social Science and understand the dynamics of broken families and communities. Don't you think, Lord, we should leave it to them?'

But God said, '**You** give them something to eat.'

But they said again, 'We don't have the resources. Look, if we were to appeal to every member of the church to come and help, only a few would turn up.'

And God asked, 'What resources do you have?'

'Well, just us; about eight or ten usually.'

'Then', God said, 'Get started! Feed my lambs...'

And so they organised a Family Fun Day. They asked the children what they would like to do, what food they liked, what games... they involved their parents, and thought of other resources – Line Dance, Brownies, Guides... There would be face painting, crafts, computer games, a group of puppeteers, and plenty of food... You name it, they did it! It was a great day. People crowded in... And when lunchtime came,
God took the food prepared by ordinary people,
gave thanks, and gave it back to them to share around.
And, quite spontaneously, families sat down in small groups
on the floor of the church hall and ate together.
Church people and non-church people,
black and white,
old and young...
talked and laughed and celebrated together.
Barriers were broken.
And those who stayed and tidied up afterwards said,
'It was a foretaste of the banquet God has prepared for all people.'

We rejoice in our calling
to be bearers of God's hospitality;
that God gives thanks for our offerings of time and energy,
and shows us they are enough to feed a multitude!

*Maureen Edwards*

*Give thanks for*
*the communion*
*of saints*

# Readings, Hymns and Psalms 2005/6

This table of readings, hymns and psalms is largely based on the Sunday themes of the Revised Common Lectionary and has been prepared by Norman Wallwork. Major holy days and special days of prayer and observation have also been included.

Abbreviations: HP = Hymns & Psalms (1983)  Ps = Psalm

**Week beginning 28 August 2005: 22nd in Ordinary Time**
**Pride and Humility**

| S | 28 | Luke 14:1,7-14 | HP460 | Ps 112 |
|---|----|----------------|-------|--------|
| M | 29 | Isaiah 2.5-17 | HP676 | Ps 71 |
| T | 30 | Isaiah 57:14-21 | HP458 | Ps 27 |
| W | 31 | Luke 14:15-24 | HP520 | Ps 34 |
| T | 1 | 2 Chronicles 12:1-12 | HP432 | Ps 69:1-17 |
| F | 2 | Hebrews 13:7-21 | HP702 | Ps 89:1-18 |
| S | 3 | Romans 12.9-21 | HP753 | Ps 17 |

**Week beginning 4 September: 23rd in Ordinary Time**
**Faith and Community**

| S | 4 | Matthew 18.15-20 | HP691 | Ps 95 |
|---|---|------------------|-------|-------|
| M | 5 | Leviticus 4.17-31 | HP228 | Ps 62 |
| T | 6 | Leviticus 5.14-16 | HP629 | Ps 8 |
| W | 7 | Matthew 21.18-22 | HP551 | Ps 15 |
| T | 8a | Luke 1.39-47 | HP90 | Ps 45 |
| F | 9 | Romans 13.1-7 | HP424 | Ps 16 |
| S | 10 | Leviticus 16.1-5, 20-28 | HP225 | Ps 113 |

*[a = Nativity of Blessed Virgin Mary]*

**Week beginning 11 September: 24th in Ordinary Time**
**Healing and Forgiveness**

| S | 11b | Matthew 18.21-35 | HP521 | Ps 103 |
|---|-----|------------------|-------|--------|
| M | 12 | Genesis 37.12-36 | HP518 | Ps 28 |
| T | 13 | Genesis 41.53-42.17 | HP134 | Ps 101 |
| W | 14c | Philippians 2.5-11 | HP180 | Ps 22 |
| T | 15 | Matthew 6.7-15 | HP518 | Ps 31 |
| F | 16 | Romans 14.13-15.2 | HP752 | Ps 49 |
| S | 17 | Genesis 45.1-20 | HP38 | Ps 133 |

*[b = Racial Justice Sunday; c = Holy Cross Day]*

**Week beginning 18 September: 25th in Ordinary Time**
**First and Last**

| S | 18 | Matthew 20.1-16 | HP699 | Ps 145 |
|---|----|-----------------|-------|--------|
| M | 19 | Genesis 27.1-29 | HP374 | Ps 126 |
| T | 20 | Genesis 28.10-17 | HP485 | Ps 124 |
| W | 21d | Matthew 9.9-13 | HP583 | Ps 19 |
| T | 22 | Matthew 19.23-30 | HP798 | Ps 149 |
| F | 23 | Romans 16.1-20 | HP797 | Ps 43 |
| S | 24 | Isaiah 41.1-13 | HP662 | Ps 125 |

*[d = Matthew, Apostle]*

**Week beginning 25 September: 26th in Ordinary Time**
**Strength to Serve**

| S | 25 | Matthew 21.28-32 | HP513 | Ps 25 |
|---|----|------------------|-------|-------|
| M | 26 | Judges 16.1-22 | HP715 | Ps 102 |
| T | 27 | Judges 16.23-31 | HP798 | Ps 87 |
| W | 28 | Matthew 9.2-8 | HP390 | Ps 137.1-6 |
| T | 29e | John 1.47-51 | HP20 | Ps 138 |
| F | 30 | Philippians 1.3-30 | HP167 | Ps 79.1-9 |
| S | 1 | Joshua 4.1-24 | HP437 | Ps 69.31-38 |

*[e = Michael and All Angels]*

**Week beginning 2 October: 27th in Ordinary Time**
**The Lord's Vineyard**

| S | 2 | Matthew 21.33-46 | HP220 | Ps 80 |
|---|---|------------------|-------|-------|
| M | 3 | Ezekiel 19.10-14 | HP240 | Ps 122 |
| T | 4 | Isaiah 27.1-6 | HP305 | Ps 126 |
| W | 5 | John 7.40-52 | HP309 | Ps 86.1-9 |
| T | 6 | Song of Solomon 8.5-14 | HP750 | Ps 1 |
| F | 7 | 1 Peter 2.4-10 | HP485 | Ps 136 |
| S | 8 | John 15.1-8 | HP730 | Ps 139 |

**Week beginning 9 October: 28th in Ordinary Time**
**The Welcome Feast**

| S | 9 | Matthew 22.1-14 | HP139 | Ps 23 |
|---|----|------------------|-------|-------|
| M | 10 | Exodus 19.7-20 | HP236 | Ps 141 |
| T | 11 | Amos 9.5-15 | HP238 | Ps 144 |
| W | 12 | John 6.25-35 | HP620 | Ps 2 |
| T | 13 | Song of Solomon 7.10-8.4 | HP314 | Ps 130 |
| F | 14 | Philippians 3.13-4.1 | HP710 | Ps 32 |
| S | 15 | Revelation 21.22-27 | HP433 | Ps 10 |

*[Week of Prayer for World Peace]*

**Week beginning 16 October: 29th in Ordinary Time**
**God and Caesar**

| S | 16 | Matthew 22.15-22 | HP409 | Ps 96 |
|---|-----|------------------|-------|-------|
| M | 17 | Daniel 3.1-30 | HP817 | Ps 13 |
| T | 18f | 2 Timothy 4.5-17 | HP793 | Ps 145 |
| W | 19 | Matthew 17.22-27 | HP789 | Ps 124 |
| T | 20 | Deuteronomy 17.14-20 | HP786 | Ps 20 |
| F | 21 | Revelation 18.1-20 | HP783 | Ps 24 |
| S | 22 | Daniel 6.1-28 | HP772 | Ps 25 |

*[One World Week; f = Luke the Evangelist]*

**Week beginning 23 October: 30th in Ordinary Time**
**Loving our Neighbour**

| S | 23 | Matthew 22.34-40 | HP785 | Ps 18 |
|---|-----|------------------|-------|-------|
| M | 24 | Deuteronomy 6.1-25 | HP381 | Ps 68 |
| T | 25 | Deuteronomy 10.10-22 | HP687 | Ps 126 |
| W | 26 | Matthew 19.16-22 | HP378 | Ps 33 |
| T | 27 | Proverbs 16.1-20 | HP714 | Ps 34 |
| F | 28g | John 15.17-27 | HP438 | Ps 19 |
| S | 29 | James 2.8-26 | HP767 | Ps 38 |

*[g = Simon & Jude: Apostles]*

Week beginning 30 October: 31st in Ordinary Time
**Leadership and Humility**

| | | | | |
|---|---|---|---|---|
| S | 30 | Matthew 23.1-12 | HP404 | Ps 131 |
| M | 31 | 1 Samuel 2.27-36 | HP788 | Ps 139 |
| T | 1h | Revelation 7.9-17 | HP821 | Ps 24 |
| W | 2 | 1 Peter 1.3-9 | HP820 | Ps 23 |
| T | 3 | Ezekiel 13.1-16 | HP777 | Ps 145 |
| F | 4 | Matthew 23.13-28 | HP780 | Ps 147 |
| S | 5 | Malachi 1.6-2.9 | HP781 | Ps 149 |

*[h = All Saints' Day]*

Week beginning 6 November: 32nd in Ordinary Time
**Awake to Judgement**

| | | | | |
|---|---|---|---|---|
| S | 6i | Matthew 25.1-13 | HP248 | Ps 63 |
| M | 7 | Joel 1.1-14 | HP690 | Ps 86 |
| T | 8 | Joel 3.9-21 | HP817 | Ps 15 |
| W | 9 | Matthew 24.1-14 | HP663 | Ps 65 |
| T | 10 | Amos 8.7-14 | HP409 | Ps 119.89-96 |
| F | 11 | 1 Thessalonians 3.6-13 | HP661 | Ps 46 |
| S | 12 | Joshua 24.1-25 | HP670 | Ps 92 |

*[i = Methodist Homes Sunday]*

Week beginning 13 November: 33rd in Ordinary Time
**Mercy and Judgement**

| | | | | |
|---|---|---|---|---|
| S | 13j | Matthew 25.14-30 | HP566 | Ps 90 |
| M | 14 | Zechariah 1.7-17 | HP242 | Ps 79 |
| T | 15 | Zechariah 2.1-5 | HP240 | Ps 19 |
| W | 16 | Matthew 24.45-51 | HP538 | Ps 26 |
| T | 17 | Job 16.1-21 | HP429 | Ps 74 |
| F | 18 | 1 Thessalonians 4.1-12 | HP421 | Ps 137.1-6 |
| S | 19 | Judges 4.1-7 | HP475 | Ps 139 |

*[j = Remembrance Sunday]*

Week beginning 20 November: Week before Advent
**Royal Judgement**

| | | | | |
|---|---|---|---|---|
| S | 20k | Matthew 25.31-46 | HP243 | Ps 128 |
| M | 21 | Esther 2.1-18 | HP239 | Ps 13 |
| T | 22 | Esther 8.3-17 | HP793 | Ps 12 |
| W | 23 | John 5.19-40 | HP245 | Ps 1 |
| T | 24 | Ezekiel 33.7-20 | HP247 | Ps 149 |
| F | 25 | Revelation 19.1-9 | HP252 | Ps 2 |
| S | 26 | Judges 5 | HP244 | Ps 8 |

*[Prisons Week; k = Christ the King & Youth Sunday*

Week beginning 27 November: 1st of Advent
**The Day of the Lord**

| | | | | |
|---|---|---|---|---|
| S | 27 | Mark 13.24-37 | HP249 | Ps 25 |
| M | 28 | Zechariah 13.1-9 | HP75 | Ps 70 |
| T | 29 | Zechariah 14.1-9 | HP74 | Ps 50 |
| W | 30l | Matthew 4.18-22 | HP141 | Ps 19 |
| T | 1m | Matthew 24.15-31 | HP246 | Ps 28 |
| F | 2 | Micah 2.1-13 | HP432 | Ps 40 |
| S | 3 | 1 Thessalonians 4.1-18 | HP745 | Ps 9 |

*[l = Andrew, Apostle; m = World AIDS Day]*

Week beginning 4 December: 2nd of Advent
**The Path of the Righteous**

| | | | | |
|---|---|---|---|---|
| S | 4 | Mark 1.1-8 | HP237 | Ps 85 |
| M | 5 | Isaiah 26.7-15 | HP236 | Ps 75 |
| T | 6 | Isaiah 4.2-6 | HP322 | Ps 146 |
| W | 7 | Mark 11.27-33 | HP241 | Ps 76 |
| T | 8 | Malachi 2.10-3.1 | HP245 | Ps 82 |
| F | 9 | Acts 11.1-18 | HP583 | Ps 147.1-12 |
| S | 10 | Daniel 7.1-10 | HP811 | Ps 149 |

Week beginning 11 December: 3rd of Advent
**The Prophetic Voice**

| | | | | |
|---|---|---|---|---|
| S | 11 | John 1.1-6, 19-28 | HP681 | Ps 126 |
| M | 12 | 1 Kings 18.1-18 | HP227 | Ps 117 |
| T | 13 | 2 Kings 2.9-22 | HP295 | Ps 150 |
| W | 14 | Mark 9.9-13 | HP290 | Ps 147.13-20 |
| T | 15 | Malachi 3.16-4.6 | HP84 | Ps 148 |
| F | 16 | Acts 3.17-4.4 | HP83 | Ps 53 |
| S | 17 | Luke 1.47-55 | HP87 | Ps 110 |

Week beginning 18 December: 4th of Advent
**The Promised Child**

| | | | | |
|---|---|---|---|---|
| S | 18 | Luke 1.26-38 | HP86 | Ps 89 |
| M | 19 | 1 Samuel 1.1-18 | HP85 | Ps 114 |
| T | 20 | 1 Samuel 1.19-28 | HP81 | Ps 148 |
| W | 21 | Mark 11.1-11 | HP77 | Ps 147 |
| T | 22 | Judges 13.2-24 | HP89 | Ps 117 |
| F | 23 | Hebrews 8.1-13 | HP90 | Ps 149 |
| S | 24 | Hebrews 10.1-10 | HP99 | Ps 85 |

Week beginning 25 December: Christmas
**Love Incarnate**

| | | | | |
|---|---|---|---|---|
| S | 25o | John 1.1-14 | HP96 | Ps 110 |
| M | 26p | Acts 6.1-7 | HP818 | Ps 13 |
| T | 27q | John 13.21-35 | HP117 | Ps 92 |
| W | 28r | Jeremiah 31.15-17 | HP127 | Ps 124 |
| T | 29 | Isaiah 12 | HP119 | Ps 149 |
| F | 30 | Luke 2.22-35 | HP126 | Ps 96 |
| S | 31 | 1 John 2.12-17 | HP105 | Ps 45 |

*[o = Christmas Day; p = Stephen, Martyr; q = John,
Evangelist r = Holy Innocents]*

Week beginning 1 January 2006: 2nd of Christmas
**The Saving Name**

| | | | | |
|---|---|---|---|---|
| S | 1s | Luke 2.15-21 | HP80 | Ps 8 |
| M | 2 | Isaiah 42.1-9 | HP78 | Ps 146 |
| T | 3 | Ephesians 1.15-23 | HP74 | Ps 111 |
| W | 4 | Philippians 2.5-11 | HP264 | Ps 112 |
| T | 5 | Acts 3.1-16 | HP271 | Ps 150 |
| F | 6t | Isaiah 49.1-6 | HP122 | Ps 72 |
| S | 7 | John 8.39-59 | HP123 | Ps 21 |

*[s = Naming of Jesus & Covenant; t = Epiphany]*

Week beginning 8 January: 1st in Ordinary Time
**The Waters of Salvation**

| | | | | |
|---|---|---|---|---|
| S | 8u | Mark 1.4-11 | HP132 | Ps 29 |
| M | 9 | Exodus 14.26-30 | HP194 | Ps 69 |
| T | 10 | Joshua 3.14-17 | HP437 | Ps 136 |
| W | 11 | John 3.1-16 | HP668 | Ps 119.65-80 |
| T | 12 | Isaiah 41.14-20 | HP616 | Ps 116 |
| F | 13 | Acts 22.2-16 | HP582 | Ps 76 |
| S | 14 | Mark 10.35-45 | HP583 | Ps 130 |

*[u = Sunday after the Epiphany; The Baptism of Christ]*

Week beginning 15 January: 2nd in Ordinary Time
**Calling and Vocation**

| | | | | |
|---|---|---|---|---|
| S | 15 | John 1.43-51 | HP696 | Ps 97 |
| M | 16 | 1 Samuel 9.27-10.8 | HP 698 | Ps 18.1-16 |
| T | 17 | 1 Samuel 15.10-31 | HP 748 | Ps 18.17-31 |
| W | 18v | Luke 18.15-17 | HP 146 | Ps 139 |
| T | 19 | Genesis 16.1-15 | HP 432 | Ps 42 |
| F | 20 | 2 Corinthians 6.14-7.1 | HP 701 | Ps 43 |
| S | 21 | Jeremiah 1.4-10 | HP 703 | Ps 44 |

*[v = Octave of Prayer for Unity begins]*

Week beginning 22 January: 3rd in Ordinary Time
**Vocation and Providence**

| | | | | |
|---|---|---|---|---|
| S | 22 | Mark 1.14-20 | HP141 | Ps 100 |
| M | 23 | Genesis 12.1-9 | HP662 | Ps 99 |
| T | 24 | Mark 3.13-19 | HP378 | Ps 112 |
| W | 25w | Galatians 1.11-24 | HP799 | Ps 18 |
| T | 26 | Proverbs 8.1-21 | HP674 | Ps 148 |
| F | 27x | 1 Corinthians 7.17-24 | HP303 | Ps 20 |
| S | 28 | Genesis 45.25-46.7 | HP310 | Ps 21.1-7 |

*[w = Conversion of St. Paul; x = Holocaust Memorial Day]*

Week beginning 29 January: 4th in Ordinary Time
**The Power of the Word**

| | | | | |
|---|---|---|---|---|
| S | 29 | Mark 1.21-28 | HP148 | Ps 111 |
| M | 30 | Numbers 22.1-21 | HP147 | Ps 45 |
| T | 31 | Numbers 22.22-38 | HP423 | Ps 46 |
| W | 1 | Mark 5.1-20 | HP395 | Ps 47 |
| T | 2y | Luke 2.22-32 | HP126 | Ps 24 |
| F | 3 | Jeremiah 29.1-14 | HP467 | Ps 74.1-12 |
| S | 4 | 1 Corinthians 7.32-40 | HP367 | Ps 74.12-23 |

*[y = Presentation of Christ in the Temple, Candlemas]*

Week beginning 5 February: 5th in Ordinary Time
**A Healing Presence**

| | | | | |
|---|---|---|---|---|
| S | 5z | Mark 1.29-39 | HP391 | Ps 147 |
| M | 6 | 2 Kings 4.8-17, 32-37 | HP290 | Ps 6 |
| T | 7 | 2 Kings 8.1-6 | HP291 | Ps 76 |
| W | 8 | Mark 3.7-12 | HP297 | Ps 78 |
| T | 9 | Job 6.1-13 | HP541 | Ps 80 |
| F | 10 | 1 Corinthians 9.1-16 | HP544 | Ps 81 |
| S | 11 | Luke 8.40-56 | HP390 | Ps 84 |

*[z = Education Sunday]*

Week beginning 12 February: 6th in Ordinary Time
**A Healing God**

| | | | | |
|---|---|---|---|---|
| S | 12 | Mark 1.40-45 | HP397 | Ps 35 |
| M | 13 | Leviticus 13.1-17 | HP398 | Ps 85 |
| T | 14 | Leviticus 14.1-20 | HP139 | Ps 86 |
| W | 15 | John 4.46-54 | HP393 | Ps 92 |
| T | 16 | Job 30.16-31 | HP544 | Ps 98 |
| F | 17 | Acts 3. 1-10 | HP5 | Ps 102 |
| S | 18 | Acts 5.12-16 | HP399 | Ps 6 |

Week beginning 19 February: 7th in Ordinary Time
**Restored and Redeemed**

| | | | | |
|---|---|---|---|---|
| S | 19 | Mark 2.1-12 | HP217 | Ps 41 |
| M | 20 | Isaiah 30.18-26 | HP13 | Ps 13 |
| T | 21 | Micah 4.1-7 | HP16 | Ps 18 |
| W | 22 | John 5.19-29 | HP46 | Ps 19 |
| T | 23 | Acts 14.8-18 | HP49 | Ps 12 |
| F | 24 | 2 Corinthians 1.1-11 | HP53 | Ps 33 |
| S | 25 | Acts 19.11-20 | HP56 | Ps 38 |

Week beginning 26 February: Week before Lent
**Glory and Sacrifice**

| | | | | |
|---|---|---|---|---|
| S | 26 | Mark 9.2-9 | HP156 | Ps 50 |
| M | 27 | Exodus 19.7-25 | HP158 | Ps 144 |
| T | 28 | Job 19.23-27 | HP196 | Ps 146 |
| W | 1aa | Matthew 6.1-21 | HP130 | Ps 6 |
| T | 2 | Daniel 9.1-14 | HP533 | Ps 7 |
| F | 3 | Daniel 9.15-25a | HP484 | Ps 32 |
| S | 4 | Hebrews 2.5-13 | HP663 | Ps 51 |

*[aa = Ash Wednesday]*

Week beginning 5 March: 1st in Lent
**Temptation and Deliverance**

| | | | | |
|---|---|---|---|---|
| S | 5 | Mark 1.9-15 | HP68 | Ps 25 |
| M | 6 | Job 4.1-21 | HP583 | Ps 40 |
| T | 7 | Job 5.8-27 | HP728 | Ps 130 |
| W | 8 | Matthew 4.1-11 | HP132 | Ps 131 |
| T | 9 | Proverbs 30.1-9 | HP131 | Ps 31 |
| F | 10ab | 1 Peter 3.8-18a | HP510 | Ps 77 |
| S | 11 | Hebrews 5 | HP381 | Ps 39 |

*[ab = World Day of Prayer]*

Week beginning 12 March: 2nd in Lent
**The Call to Faith**

| | | | | |
|---|---|---|---|---|
| S | 12 | Mark 8.31-38 | HP221 | Ps 22 |
| M | 13 | Genesis 21.1-7 | HP670 | Ps 77 |
| T | 14 | Genesis 22.1-19 | HP672 | Ps 30 |
| W | 15 | Mark 10.32-34 | HP224 | Ps 39 |
| T | 16 | Jeremiah 30.12-22 | HP767 | Ps 102 |
| F | 17 | Hebrews 11.1-19 | HP675 | Ps 139 |
| S | 18ac | Matthew 1.18-25 | HP383 | Ps 132 |

*[ac = Joseph of Nazareth]*

Week beginning 19 March: 3rd in Lent
**The Temple**

| | | | | |
|---|---|---|---|---|
| S | 19 | John 2.13-22 | HP485 | Ps 19 |
| M | 20 | 1 Kings 6.1-22 | HP484 | Ps 22.1-21 |
| T | 21 | 2 Chronicles 29.1-19 | HP487 | Ps 22.22-31 |
| W | 22 | Mark 11.15-19 | HP490 | Ps 15 |
| T | 23 | Ezra 6.1-16 | HP494 | Ps 23 |
| F | 24 | 1 Corinthians 3.10-23 | HP267 | Ps 38 |
| S | 25 | Galatians 4.1-7 | HP87 | Ps 113 |

*[ad = Annunciation of the Lord]*

Week beginning 26 March: 4th in Lent
**Exalting the Cross**

| | | | | |
|---|---|---|---|---|
| S | 26ae | John 3.14-21 | HP219 | Ps 107 |
| M | 27 | Exodus 15.22-27 | HP273 | Ps 140 |
| T | 28 | Numbers 20.1-13 | HP174 | Ps 86 |
| W | 29 | John 8.12-20 | HP681 | Ps 94 |
| T | 30 | Isaiah 60.15-20 | HP455 | Ps 104 |
| F | 31 | Hebrews 3.1-6 | HP822 | Ps 6 |
| S | 1 | Colossians 1.15-20 | HP165 | Ps 84 |

*[ae = Mothering Sunday]*

Week beginning 2 April: 5th in Lent
**Life through Death**

| | | | | |
|---|---|---|---|---|
| S | 2 | John 12.20-33 | HP231 | Ps 119.9-16 |
| M | 3 | Isaiah 43.8-13 | HP235 | Ps 88 |
| T | 4 | Isaiah 44.1-8 | HP233 | Ps 122,123 |
| W | 5 | John 12.34-50 | HP229 | Ps 130,131 |
| T | 6 | Haggai 2.1-23 | HP174 | Ps 147 |
| F | 7 | 2 Corinthians 3.4-11 | HP175 | Ps 18.1-16 |
| S | 8 | Luke 22.24-28 | HP176 | Ps 18.17-31 |

Week beginning 9 April: Holy Week
**Obedient unto Death**

| | | | | |
|---|---|---|---|---|
| S | 9af | Mark 14.21-32 | HP176 | Ps 31 |
| M | 10 | Lamentation 1.1-12 | HP178 | Ps 42 |
| T | 11 | Lamentations 3.1-18 | HP180 | Ps 43 |
| W | 12 | Jeremiah 11.18-20 | HP217 | Ps 116 |
| T | 13ag | 1 Corinthians 11.23b-35 | HP614 | Ps 23 |
| F | 14ah | Isaiah 53 | HP225 | Ps 22 |
| S | 15ai | Mark 15.42-47 | HP583 | Ps 30 |

*[af = Palm Sunday; ag = Maundy Thursday;*
*ah = Good Friday; ai = Holy Saturday]*

Week beginning 16 April: Easter Week
**Christ is Risen! Alleluia!**

| | | | | |
|---|---|---|---|---|
| S | 16aj | Mark 16.1-8 | HP193 | Ps 118 |
| M | 17 | Genesis 1.1-2.4a | HP195 | Ps 114 |
| T | 18 | Isaiah 26.1-19 | HP196 | Ps 111 |
| W | 19 | Luke 24.1-12 | HP192 | Ps 118 |
| T | 20 | Revelation 1.4-18 | HP194 | Ps 16 |
| F | 21 | 1 Corinthians 15.1-11 | HP190 | Ps 116,117 |
| S | 22 | Matthew 28.1-7 | HP188 | Ps 121 |

*[aj = Easter Day]*

Week beginning 23 April: 2nd of Easter
**God with us**

| | | | | |
|---|---|---|---|---|
| S | 23 | John 20.19-31 | HP205 | Ps 122 |
| M | 24 | Daniel 3.1-30 | HP207 | Ps 123 |
| T | 25ak | 2 Timothy 4.1-11 | HP468 | Ps 45 |
| W | 26 | Daniel 6.1-28 | HP191 | Ps 124 |
| T | 27 | Mark 12.18-27 | HP187 | Ps 125 |
| F | 28 | 1 John 2.3-17 | HP202 | Ps 126 |
| S | 29 | Isaiah 26.1-15 | HP198 | Ps 127 |

*[ak = Mark, Evangelist]*

Week beginning 30 April: 3rd of Easter
**Fellowship with the Risen Christ**

| | | | | |
|---|---|---|---|---|
| S | 30 | Luke 24.36b-48 | HP 610 | Ps 4 |
| M | 1al | John 12.20-26 | HP 781 | Ps 27 |
| T | 2 | Daniel 10.2-9 | HP 601 | Ps 30 |
| W | 3 | Mark 16.9-18 | HP 186 | Ps 57 |
| T | 4 | Hosea 5.15-6.6 | HP 204 | Ps 113 |
| F | 5 | 1 John 3.7-15 | HP 568 | Ps 103 |
| S | 6 | Jeremiah 30.1-11a | HP 425 | Ps 128 |

*[al = Philip & James, Apostles]*

Week beginning 7 May: 4th of Easter
**The Good Shepherd**

| | | | | |
|---|---|---|---|---|
| S | 7 | John 10.11-18 | HP263 | Ps 23 |
| M | 8 | Genesis 48.8-19 | HP767 | Ps 133 |
| T | 9 | 1 Chronicles 11.1-9 | HP69 | Ps 135 |
| W | 10 | Mark 14.26-31 | HP43 | Ps 136 |
| T | 11 | Micah 7.8-20 | HP678 | Ps 145 |
| F | 12 | 1 Peter 5.1-5 | HP772 | Ps 146 |
| S | 13 | Ezekiel 34.11-16 | HP750 | Ps 95 |

Week beginning 14 May: 5th of Easter
**The Lord's Vineyard**

| | | | | |
|---|---|---|---|---|
| S | 14am | John 15.1-8 | HP730 | Ps 22 |
| M | 15 | Isaiah 5.1-7 | HP766 | Ps 110 |
| T | 16 | Isaiah 32.9-20 | HP763 | Ps 111 |
| W | 17 | John 14.18-31 | HP761 | Ps 112 |
| T | 18 | Isaiah 65.17-25 | HP768 | Ps 116 |
| F | 19 | Galatians 5.16-26 | HP777 | Ps 129 |
| S | 20 | Isaiah 12.1-6 | HP783 | Ps 132 |

*[am = Christian Aid Week]*

Week beginning 21 May: 6th of Easter
**The Gifts of the Ascending Christ**

| | | | | |
|---|---|---|---|---|
| S | 21 | John 15.9-17 | HP211 | Ps 98 |
| M | 22 | Acts 10.44-48 | HP209 | Ps 147 |
| T | 23 | Mark 16.19-20 | HP210 | Ps 148 |
| W | 24an | Romans 5.1-11 | HP744 | Ps 130 |
| T | 25ao | Acts 1.1-11 | HP197 | Ps 47 |
| F | 26 | Revelation 1.9-18 | HP201 | Ps 24 |
| S | 27 | Philippians 2.5-11 | HP206 | Ps 15 |

*[an = Conversion of John Wesley; ao = Ascension]*

## Week beginning 28 May: 1st after Ascension
### The Intercession of Christ

| | | | | |
|---|---|---|---|---|
| S | 28 | John 17.6-19 | HP622 | Ps 1 |
| M | 29 | Exodus 22.29-38 | HP235 | Ps 8 |
| T | 30 | Numbers 8.5-22 | HP243 | Ps 21 |
| W | 31 | John 16.16-24 | HP262 | Ps 110 |
| T | 1 | Ezra 9.5-15 | HP268 | Ps 100 |
| F | 2 | 3 John 1-15 | HP271 | Ps 20 |
| S | 3 | Romans 8.1-27 | HP279 | Ps 99 |

## Week beginning 4 June: Pentecost
### The Outpoured Spirit

| | | | | |
|---|---|---|---|---|
| S | 4ap | Acts 2.1-21 | HP307 | Ps 104 |
| M | 5 | Joel 2.18-29 | HP306 | Ps 149 |
| T | 6 | Ezekiel 37.1-14 | HP321 | Ps 48 |
| W | 7 | John 7.37-39 | HP299 | Ps 145 |
| T | 8 | Genesis 11.1-9 | HP290 | Ps 46 |
| F | 9 | 1 Corinthians 12.4-27 | HP289 | Ps 48 |
| S | 10 | Romans 8.22-27 | HP296 | Ps 33 |

[ap = Pentecost, Whitsunday]

## Week beginning 11 June: Trinity
### The Blessed Trinity

| | | | | |
|---|---|---|---|---|
| S | 11aq | John 3.1-17 | HP6 | Ps 29 |
| M | 12ar | Acts 14.8-20 | HP820 | Ps 19 |
| T | 13 | Numbers 9.15-23 | HP7 | Ps 100 |
| W | 14 | Exodus 3.1-6 | HP18 | Ps 93 |
| T | 15 | Revelation 4 | HP791 | Ps 33 |
| F | 16 | Mark 1.1-13 | HP519 | Ps 115 |
| S | 17 | Exodus 34.1-10 | HP29 | Ps 149 |

[aq = Trinity Sunday; ar = Barnabas, Apostle; World Refugee Week]

## Week beginning 18 June: 11th in Ordinary Time
### The Tree of Life

| | | | | |
|---|---|---|---|---|
| S | 18 | Mark 4.26-34 | HP781 | Ps 20 |
| M | 19 | John 3.11-15 | HP228 | Ps 3 |
| T | 20 | John 19.25-30 | HP175 | Ps 5 |
| W | 21 | 1 Peter 2.18-25 | HP216 | Ps 10 |
| T | 22 | Genesis 3.14-24 | HP223 | Ps 28 |
| F | 23 | Revelation 21.22-22.5 | HP231 | Ps 41 |
| S | 24as | Luke 3.1-17 | HP819 | Ps 50 |

[as = John the Baptist]

## Week beginning 25 June: 12th in Ordinary Time
### The Waters of Salvation

| | | | | |
|---|---|---|---|---|
| S | 25 | Mark 4.35-41 | HP144 | Ps 107 |
| M | 26 | Exodus 7.14-24 | HP528 | Ps 100 |
| T | 27 | Exodus 9.13-35 | HP684 | Ps 29 |
| W | 28 | Mark 6.45-52 | HP269 | Ps 93 |
| T | 29at | Acts 3.1-10 | HP257 | Ps 124 |
| F | 30 | Acts 27.13-38 | HP65 | Ps 121 |
| S | 1 | Joshua 10.1-14 | HP261 | Ps 46 |

[at = Peter, Apostle]

## Week beginning 2 July: 13th in Ordinary Time
### The Faithfulness of God

| | | | | |
|---|---|---|---|---|
| S | 2 | Mark 5.21-43 | HP66 | Ps 130 |
| M | 3au | John 11.1-16 | HP583 | Ps 92 |
| T | 4 | Hosea 11.1-12 | HP51 | Ps 5 |
| W | 5 | Mark 9.14-29 | HP743 | Ps 10 |
| T | 6 | 2 Kings 20.1-11 | HP13 | Ps 42 |
| F | 7 | 2 Corinthians 7.2-16 | HP38 | Ps 49 |
| S | 8 | Jonah 2.1-10 | HP356 | Ps 88 |

[au = Thomas the Apostle]

## Week beginning 9 July: 14th in Ordinary Time
### The Great Commission

| | | | | |
|---|---|---|---|---|
| S | 9av | Mark 6.1-13 | HP768 | Ps 48 |
| M | 10 | Jeremiah 16.1-13 | HP770 | Ps 52 |
| T | 11 | Jeremiah 16.14-21 | HP774 | Ps 56 |
| W | 12 | John 7.1-9 | HP775 | Ps 61 |
| T | 13 | Ezekiel 2.8-3.11 | HP777 | Ps 63.1-9 |
| F | 14 | 2 Corinthians 11.16-33 | HP784 | Ps 90 |
| S | 15 | Matthew 28.16-20 | HP785 | Ps 119.81-88 |

[av = NCH Sunday]

## Week beginning 16 July: 15th in Ordinary Time
### The Company of Martyrs

| | | | | |
|---|---|---|---|---|
| S | 16 | Mark 6.14-29 | HP 808 | Ps 24 |
| M | 17 | Amos 2.6-16 | HP 810 | Ps 71 |
| T | 18 | Acts 7.54-60 | HP 818 | Ps 136 |
| W | 19 | Acts 12.1-5 | HP 821 | Ps 137 |
| T | 20 | Acts 23.12-35 | HP 820 | Ps 138 |
| F | 21 | Revelation 21.1-7 | HP 823 | Ps 139 |
| S | 22aw | Luke 8.1-3 | HP 42 | Ps 150 |

[aw – Mary Magdalene]

## Week beginning 23 July: 16th in Ordinary Time
### Shepherding the Flock

| | | | | |
|---|---|---|---|---|
| S | 23 | Mark 6.30-56 | HP706 | Ps 8 |
| M | 24 | Jeremiah 50.1-7 | HP772 | Ps 12.1-7 |
| T | 25ax | Mark 10.35-45 | HP583 | Ps 29 |
| W | 26 | Luke 15.1-7 | HP460 | Ps 15 |
| T | 27 | Zechariah 9.14-10.12 | HP263 | Ps 20 |
| F | 28 | Acts 20.16-38 | HP750 | Ps 21 |
| S | 29 | 2 Samuel 5.1-12 | HP185 | Ps 24 |

[ax = James the Apostle]

## Week beginning 30 July: 17th in Ordinary Time
### The Lord's Banquet

| | | | | |
|---|---|---|---|---|
| S | 30 | John 6.1-21 | HP467 | Ps 14 |
| M | 31 | Genesis 18.1-14 | HP571 | Ps 25 |
| T | 1 | Exodus 24.1-11 | HP437 | Ps 26 |
| W | 2 | John 6.24-34 | HP599 | Ps 29 |
| T | 3 | Isaiah 25.6-10 | HP730 | Ps 42 |
| F | 4 | Philippians 4.10-20 | HP713 | Ps 43 |
| S | 5 | Isaiah 2.1-4 | HP440 | Ps 81 |

**Week beginning 6 August: 18th in Ordinary Time**
**Come and Eat**

| | | | | |
|---|---|---|---|---|
| S | 6ay | 1 John 3.1-3 | HP156 | Ps 27 |
| M | 7 | Numbers 11.16-32 | HP12 | Ps 47 |
| T | 8 | Deuteronomy 8.1-20 | HP14 | Ps 48 |
| W | 9 | Mark 8.1-10 | HP26 | Ps 54 |
| T | 10 | Isaiah 55.1-9 | HP33 | Ps 68.1-18 |
| F | 11 | Ephesians 4.17-24 | HP35 | Ps 72 |
| S | 12 | Isaiah 65.17-25 | HP40 | Ps 74.1-12 |

*[ay = The Transfiguration]*

**Week beginning 13 August: 19th in Ordinary Time**
**Nourishment for the Journey**

| | | | | |
|---|---|---|---|---|
| S | 13 | John 6.35, 41-51 | HP41 | Ps 130 |
| M | 14 | 1 Kings 17.1-16 | HP43 | Ps 76 |
| T | 15 | Ruth 2.1-23 | HP361 | Ps 80 |
| W | 16 | John 6.35-40 | HP48 | Ps 137 |
| T | 17 | Jeremiah 31.1-6 | HP50 | Ps 142 |
| F | 18 | Ephesians 5.1-14 | HP52 | Ps 143 |
| S | 19 | Acts 4.8-20 | HP56 | Ps 81 |

**Week beginning 20 August: 20th in Ordinary Time**
**Food and Famine**

| | | | | |
|---|---|---|---|---|
| S | 20 | John 6.51-58 | HP59 | Ps 111 |
| M | 21 | Genesis 43.1-15 | HP60 | Ps 121 |
| T | 22 | Genesis 45.1-15 | HP63 | Ps 124 |
| W | 23 | Mark 8.14-21 | HP64 | Ps 125 |
| T | 24 | Genesis 47. 13-26 | HP72 | Ps 128 |
| F | 25 | Acts 6.1-7 | HP334 | Ps 131 |
| S | 26 | 1 Corinthians 13.1-13 | HP301 | Ps 36 |

**Week beginning 27 August: 21st in Ordinary Time**
**Bread of Heaven**

| | | | | |
|---|---|---|---|---|
| S | 27 | John 6.56-69 | HP335 | Ps 80 |
| M | 28 | Nehemiah 9.1-15 | HP336 | Ps 132 |
| T | 29 | Nehemiah 9.16-31 | HP338 | Ps 133 |
| W | 30 | John 15.16-25 | HP341 | Ps 135 |
| T | 31 | Isaiah 33.10-16 | HP343 | Ps 118 |
| F | 1 | Ephesians 5.21-6.9 | HP345 | Ps 119.1-16 |
| S | 2 | Colossians 2.16-19 | HP347 | Ps 119.17-32 |

## For further information

**Called to Prayer** – a companion to the Prayer Handbook which includes a selection of prayers from past years and arranges them under the themes of 'Our Calling'. *Price: £9.75 from mph.*

**The Methodist Website** www.methodist.org.uk – *includes prayers from the Prayer Handbook and other prayers.*

**Magnet** – the magazine of the Women's Network – *available from your local church or circuit distributor. Details of individual subscriptions from the Women's Network Office, Methodist Church House (MCH), 25 Marylebone Road, London NW1 5JR. Tel: 020 7486 5502.*

**Mission Matters** – part of the Link Mailing – *available from mph.*

**Words for Today** (IBRA) – reflections on daily Bible readings from many parts of the world and well-known writers.

**Light for our Path** (IBRA) – notes for those who need a simpler and less provocative approach. *Both are available from mph.*

**The Methodist Recorder** – *from your newsagent or from 122 Golden Lane, London EC1Y 0TL.*

**The Prayer Handbook on Tape** – *from Galloways Society for the Blind, Howick House, Howick Park Avenue, Penwortham, Preston PR1 0LS. Tel: 01772 753705.*

**Prayer Focus** – The Prayer Handbook of the Methodist Church in Ireland – *available from the Methodist Church in Ireland, No 9 Resources Centre, 9 Lennoxvale, Belfast BT9 5BY.*

**Copyright** – prayers in this book are © 2005 Trustees for Methodist Church Purposes, unless otherwise indicated. Churches are free to use them in public worship and reproduce up to ten prayers in magazines or newletters during the year providing acknowledgement is given.

Printed by **Swan Print and Design**, Shuttleworth Road, Elms Farm Industrial Estate, Bedford MK41 0EP.

**Key** – The letters beside the names indicate the type of work in which Mission Partners are mainly engaged:

| | |
|---|---|
| ad | administration |
| ag | agriculture |
| d | doctor |
| ed | education |
| m | medical work (other than doctor or nurse) |
| n | nurse |
| p | pastoral worker |
| rt | retired |
| sd | social/development work |
| sp | special partner |
| t | technical |
| th | theological training |
| o | minister |
| * | deacon |
| + | **Joint Appointment** |
| USPG | United Society for the Propagation of the Gospel (Anglican) |
| CMS | Church Mission Society (Anglican) |
| CofS | Church of Scotland |
| CA | Christians Abroad |
| NMA | Nationals in Mission Appointments |
| UCA | United College of the Ascension |
| WCBP | World Church in Britain Partnership |

# An outline for Morning and Evening Prayer

Open our lips, O Lord,
**And we shall praise your name.**
Glory to the Father, and to the Son,
and to the Holy Spirit:
**As it was in the beginning, is now,
and shall be for ever. Amen**

(From Easter to Pentecost: **Alleluia**)

**Hymn ***

**Psalm *** and *Glory to the Father*

**Scripture ***

**Canticle from *Hymns & Psalms***

| Morning | | Evening | |
|---|---|---|---|
| S | 825 | S | 826 |
| M | 833 | M | 828 |
| T | 824 | T | 831 |
| W | 832 | W | 829 |
| T | 831 | T | 830 |
| F | 829 | F | 644 |
| S | 830 | S | 832 |

**The Lord's Prayer**

**Collect of the Day or of the Week**

**Morning Collect**
Lord our God, as with all creation, we offer you the life of this new day; give us grace to love and serve you to the praise of Jesus Christ our Lord. Amen

**Evening Collect**
Lord our God, at the ending of this day, and in the darkness and silence of this night, cover us with healing and forgiveness, that we may take our rest in peace, through Jesus Christ our Lord. Amen

**Thanksgiving**

**Intercession**

**The Grace**

* See Lectionary

# An outline for a Preaching Service

**Welcome and Call to Worship**

**Hymn**

**Prayers:**

    **Invocation or Adoration**

    **Confession**

    **Declaration of Forgiveness**

    **Collect of the Day**

**Hymn**

**Old Testament Lesson**

**Psalm**

**Lesson from the Apostles (Epistle)**

**Hymn**

**Lesson from the Gospels**

**Sermon**

**Hymn**

**Prayers**

    **Thanksgiving** (for Creation, Redemption in Christ and the life of the Church in the Spirit);

    **Intercession*** (for the Church and its mission; for the world and its communities; for the sick and those in need; specific petitions and remembrance of those who have died).

    **The Lord's Prayer**

**Notices**

**Offering and Prayer at the Offering**

**Hymn**

**Blessing and Dismissal**

* *Including relevant day in Prayer Handbook*